CISTERCIAN STUDIES SERIES: NUMBER FIFTY-SIX

THE OCCUPATION OF CELTIC SITES
IN MEDIEVAL IRELAND
BY THE CANONS REGULAR OF ST AUGUSTINE
AND THE CISTERCIANS

CISTERCIAN STUDIES SERIES: NUMBER FIFTY-SIX

THE OCCUPATION OF CELTIC SITES IN MEDIEVAL IRELAND BY THE CANONS REGULAR OF ST AUGUSTINE AND THE CISTERCIANS

by

GERALDINE CARVILLE

Cistercian Publications
Kalamazoo, Michigan
1982

Available in Britain and Europe from
A.R. Mowbray & Co., Ltd., St Thomas House
Becket Street, Oxford   OX1 1SJ

Typeset by the Carmelites of Indianapolis

Library of Congress Cataloguing in Publication Data

Carville, Geraldine.
   The occupation of Celtic sites in medieval Ireland by the Canons Regular of
St. Augustine and the Cistercians.
      (Cistercian studies series; 56)
      1. Augustinian Canons—Ireland.   2. Cistercians—Ireland.
3. Abbeys—Ireland.   4. Ecclesiastical geography—Ireland.
5. Ireland—Church history—Medieval period, 600–1500.   6. Celts—
Ireland.   I. Title.   II. Series.
BX29.Z5I733   1982   271'.12'0415   82–14569
   ISBN 0–87907–856–1

Contents

FOREWORD   vii

The Celtic System   3

The Augustinians   8

The Cistercians   12

The Distribution of Medieval Augustinian and
   Cistercian Abbeys   15

   General Distribution   16
      Siting in relation to population distribution   18
      Siting in relation to communications:
         Roads–Rivers   22
      Problems of classification of the physical sites
      of medieval abbeys   25

         River Valley Sitings   27
            Water Requirements   29
            Solid Foundations   49
            Building Stone   53
            Human Factors Influencing the Choice
               of Sites   56

         Islands in Lakes, Bogs, or Islands in the Sea   59
            Islands in Lakes   59
            Islands in Bogs   63
            Islands in the Sea   70

         Abbey Sites on Drumlins   71

         Miscellaneous Sites   80
            Coastal   81
            Hill Slopes   87

Conclusions   93

vi

Appendix A   95

Appendix B   107

Appendix C   112

Tables   113

Illustrations   133

Foreword

Cistercian scholars in North America were introduced to
Geraldine Carville's work in 1976, when she travelled to
Kalamazoo to present a paper at the sixth annual Conference on Cistercian Studies, held in conjunction with the
Medieval Studies Congress at Western Michigan University. As an organizer of the Cistercian Conference, I met
Ms Carville at the airport and, during the drive to cam-
pus, told her something of what she might expect during
the massive three day gathering. Her reaction then, and
throughout the Conference, was simple awe. What, she
wondered aloud at frequent intervals, was a simple geographer doing amongst the historians, theologians, and
philosophers massed at Kalamazoo. And what, some of
them were wondering silently to themselves, could a geographer possibly have to say about medieval monks.

The answer came resoundingly on the final day of the
Conference, when Ms Carville, a slide projector control in
either hand, took the podium. Her noteless presentation of
the siting of cistercian monasteries in medieval Ireland
stunned her audience. Scholars jaded after having listened
to nine papers a day for almost three full days sat up in fas-
cination. Many of us, having never so much as thought of
the practical problems involved in the cistercian explosion

of the twelfth century, learned an entirely new vocabulary and gained increased respect for the good sense and hard work of the medieval Cistercians. The landscape of Ireland and the terminology of geographers, both graphically illustrated in well-chosen slides ably explained, became familiar in twenty short minutes. The applause at the conclusion of her lecture told conference participants in nearby rooms that something quite unusual had taken place among the 'Cistercianologists'. We learned later that Ms Carville had also received the offer of a teaching fellowship on the spot.

At the repeated urgings of the Institute of Cistercian Studies, Ms Carville was persuaded five years later to share her unique insights with North Americans once again. In the autumn of 1981, she undertook a speaking tour of cistercian monasteries in the United States. Her command of her subject, her enthusiasm for all aspects of the cistercian past, and her irish good humor captivated her monastic audiences as it had scholars, and introduced many monks and nuns to an aspect of their history which has been greatly ignored.

In publishing this study, Cistercian Publications hopes to extend this awareness yet more widely. Because Ms Carville wrote as an Irishwoman and a geographer for her countrymen and colleagues, her work includes references and terminology which may not be immediately significant to others. We have therefore asked her to provide two additional maps: one showing present-day county divisions; and the other showing the physical geography of Ireland. The accumulation of photographs and the creation of maps are Ms Carville's work. Both she and the editors wish to express their appreciation to the following institutions, who have cooperated in providing materials:

The Irish Manuscripts Commission, Dublin
The Northern Irish Tourist Board
The University of Cambridge
The Ulster Museum

Geraldine Carville, a Fellow of the Royal Geographical Society, teaches in Belfast and is a Trustee of the Ulster Folk Museum. Her other works include *The Heritage of Holy Cross, Norman Splendour* (Duiske Abbey), and *Chorus Sancti Benedicti* (Middleton, Co. Cork), as well as numerous articles.

E. Rozanne Elder
Editorial Director

Ninety-six abbeys of the Order of Canons Regular of St. Augustine[1] and thirty-four abbeys of the Cistercian Order[2] existed in Medieval Ireland (See Map 1). Only abbeys or priories[3] properly so called have been shown, and cells or religious houses subordinate to these abbeys or priories have been deliberately excluded. This work attempts to explain the occupation of the Celtic sites by the Cistercians and the Canons Regular of St. Augustine in Medieval Ireland.

THE DISTRIBUTION OF CISTERCIAN AND CANONS REGULAR OF ST AUGUSTINE ABBEYS IN
MEDIAEVAL IRELAND.

MAP 1

1

Tables 1a and 1b distinguish between abbeys which were newly established and those which were located on Celtic sites for the Canons Regular of St. Augustine and Cistercians respectively. The former indicates that there was Celtic influence at fifty-seven out of ninety-six sites and at thirteen out of thirty-four in the latter case. They also denote the physical characteristics of the sites.

CANONS REGULAR

	Rivers	Islands Lake, Sea, Bog	Drumlins	Miscel-laneous	Total
Celtic	17	10	5	6	38
Celtic (Abandoned)	10	5	2	2	19
New	29	3	2	5	39

TABLE 1A

CISTERCIANS

	Rivers	Islands Lake, Sea, Bog	Drumlins	Miscel-laneous	Total
Celtic and (Celtic-Benedictine)	5	0	0	1	8
Celtic (Abandoned)	3	1	0	1	5
New	17	0	1	3	21

TABLE 1B

Some abbeys were founded on abandoned Celtic sites (See Map 2), others involved a transfer of allegiance from an existing Celtic house to the Augustinian or Cistercian rule.

MAP 2

THE CELTIC SYSTEM

An understanding of the Celtic system is essential to the study of the distribution of Augustinian and Cistercian medieval abbeys because so many of them were established on Celtic sites, and in houses still inhabited by Celtic monks a transference from their rule to that of the new orders took place (See Map 3 and 4). In view of this strong relationship it is vital to have some understanding of the Celtic system.

4

MAP 3

(FOR DETAILS OF THIS MAP SEE TABLE NO. 1, P. 2)

MAP 4

CELTIC COMMUNITY TRANSFERS TO THE CISTERCIAN ORDER
FOR DETAILS SEE TABLE 4, P. 123

Down to the fifth century AD Ireland was pagan. Shortly afterwards Pope Celestine sent Bishop Paladius to the small colonies of Christians in south east Ireland. In 432 Patrick, later St. Patrick, came to Ireland, and it was during his lifetime that one of the first monastic settlements took place on the south east coast at Dair Inis,[5] Co. Waterford. During the sixth and seventh centuries Celtic monasticism grew rapidly and took on a missionary aspect. Two outstanding monks of this period were St. Finnian of Clonard and St. Enda of Aran. The former in particular by the founding of the great monastic school of Clonard which is said to have numbered its pupils in thousands came to exercise a great influence over the whole of Ireland and became popularly known as the teacher of the saints of Ireland. Twelve of the best known monastic founders were later grouped together by hagiographers under the title of 'the twelve Apostles of Ireland' and were credited with having received their monastic education at the school of Clonard. Available evidence goes to show that many of the so-called 'Twelve Apostles of Ireland' could not have been pupils of St. Finnian of Clonard; some of them had died long before his time, while others were not born until after his death. Nevertheless the legend thus recorded bears witness to the great influence exercised by St. Finnian in the Ireland of his day.

Each monastery was independent and exercised control over a number of scattered daughter-houses. None of the Celtic monasteries derived much benefit from the ecclesiastical organisation itself before 1152, when bishoprics were created. Some monks bore the title of bishop. They had however no general jurisdiction over the organization of the monasteries nor any authority over their economic policies. They were concerned primarily with ritual matters such as the ordination of priests, consecration of bishops and the administration of the sacraments. Each monastic *Fine* (family) had an abbot who was responsible for the jurisdiction not only of his own abbey but also of any daughter-houses which might have been established. These required so much attention that the abbot was frequently away on circuit.

The large size of some monasteries can be explained in terms other than the processes of ecclesiastical organization. Some monasteries, such as Clonfert and Glendalough, supported groups of anchorites from whom the monastic bishops, scribes, and masters of the school were often recruited. Then, along with providing scope for religious life they fulfilled a number of ancillary functions such as running schools. Some were important pilgrimage centres, others housed penitents over long periods. Then there were the craftsmen whose workshops produced reliquaries and shrines. Hence many of the Celtic monasteries were characterised by a diverse and active population, so much so that some monks found all this activity disturbing to their religious life and decided to leave the bustle of the large monastery, often known as a *civitas*, in order to retire to secluded places. Favourite sites were small islands in nearby lakes. The population of these secluded houses so increased that new settlements were founded in other remote places, such as islands in other lakes or off the coast. In this way a hierarchy of monastic settlements developed. The ultimate size was dependent on three main circumstances: the nodality and accessibility of the monastery; the relative fame of the founder saint's tomb; and famous schools attached to monasteries. A dead founder renowned for holiness would draw crowds of pilgrims. Noteworthy centres of this kind were Clonmacnoise, Monachincha, Donaghnore, Fahan, Lismore, and Roscommon. Famous schools attached to monasteries attracted students from overseas. The Venerable Bede mentions Ireland's hospitality to the English visitor; he also talks about their going to Clonmelsh. And Map 39 (page 44) of Armagh[6] to which detailed reference will be made later, shows the Trian Saxon a special 'quarter' of that city assigned to the English.

The Celtic monastic foundations went from strength to strength until the end of the eighth century. By then the Norse raids had begun. The Norse men were principally interested in plunder.[7] The average rural settlement had little to offer and the absence of towns meant that the monasteries themselves provided the most likely source of precious metals and other valuables. At first they attacked only the coastal sites, but later they penetrated inland to those abbeys easily approached by river routes. Plunder was sometimes accompanied by deliberate destruction of monastic buildings and the slaughter of the monks. The onslaught was prolonged and the monasteries, unable to offer any effective resistance, declined in personnel, in wealth, and in importance. The Norse invasion was finally overcome when the forces of King Brian Boruma defeated them at Clontarf in 1014, though King Brian himself was killed.

Despite these two and a half centuries of attrition, Celtic monastic life survived, although impoverished and disorganised, and at the time of the Augustinian and the Cistercian foundations those communities still in existence willingly transferred their allegiance to the Augustinian and Cistercian rules. Irish monasticism was often of a severe type and the Cistercian Order probably most nearly approximated what the native Irish considered the more perfect form of monasticism, having much in common with the traditional Irish system. On the other hand, the majority of religious men of the twelfth century might have found the Cistercian Order too severe for themselves and the only alternative was the Canons Regular of St. Augustine, as the Benedictines[8] never really took root in Ireland, and only one foundation of Carthusians[9] was established there. The only two forms of religious life at that period were those of the monks and the canons. This gave an impetus to the Augustinian and Cistercian foundations during the twelfth century. Almost half of the Augustinians, thirty-eight of ninety-six were of this type[10] (SEE MAP 3,

8

p. 4 AND TABLE 1, p. 2). This fact ensured that the order rapidly displayed a broad geographical distribution. Transference to the Cistercian Order[11] was much less common; only eight foundations out of thirty-four were of this kind (SEE MAP 4, p. 4 AND TABLE 4, p. 123). This difference in the transfer rates between Augustinians and Cistercians was largely the outcome of their respective rules.

The Augustinians were expecially interested in *cura animarum* and as such were normally to be found in relatively densely populated areas. Since the larger Celtic monasteries themselves had been established close to the centres of population and these were mainly the ones that survived into the twelfth century, they were ready-made sites for the fulfilment of the Augustinian rule.[12] The Cistercians were quite different. Their order sought solitude 'far from the haunts of men', in places where their attention to prayer and the study of spiritual works could be undisturbed. In view of this, transference of rule was less likely to occur because the smaller isolated Celtic communities had largely died out by that time. Hence in a way it is surprising that as many as eight of the thirty-four Cistercian houses were involved in transfers of this kind.

THE AUGUSTINIANS

St. Augustine, from whom this Order derives its name though he did not found it, was Bishop (396–430) of Hippo, a town on the north African Mediterranean coast of what is now Tunisia. A distinct order of regular canons under the rule of St. Augustine did not become fully recognized until the eleventh century. Leo IX (1049–54) encouraged the grouping of reformed communities of regular canons as a way to restore religious discipline in a period of serious moral decline. When the clergy began to live in community and according to a Rule they were designated Canons Regular and when the Rule adopted was based on the writings of St. Augustine they became known as the Canons Regular of St. Augustine.

This study deals with a branch called The Canons Regular of St. Augustine of Arrouaise (from the name of the French mother-house), who were introduced to Ireland by St. Malachy.[13] It does not include those Augustinian canons called 'The Canons O.S.A. of the Holy Cross'[14] or Crutched Friars, nor the Premonstratensian Canons[15] who also followed the rule of St. Augustine.

To explain further the nature and distinctive spirit of such an order one may say with St. Augustine that a Canon Regular aims at two things: holiness and priestly duty (*sanctitatem et clericatum*). The time of the introduction of Regular Canons into Ireland is uncertain. St. Bernard in his *Life of St. Malachy* states that when Malachy became Bishop of Down (in 1137) he immediately, according to custom, formed *de filiis suis conventum regularum clericorum*, a community of regular clerics.[16] Sometime before 1148 he became acquainted with the religious men of Gisburn (Guisborough Priory), Yorkshire, founded for Augustinians c. 1119. Lawlor considers that this must have been the Order of St. Augustine because it was the only order of regular clerics to be recognised by the Church of Rome at that time.[17] He also suggests that the community established by Malachy under the influence of Gisburn was founded in Bangor, from which Malachy administered the Diocese of Down. 'According to his custom'[18] must mean that Malachy was in the habit of forming clerics into religious communities, and one therefore presumes that others were established in Ireland even before 1137. This timing is supported by Ware who places the coming of the Augustinians to Cork at c. 1134. This house is said to have been established from Cong, which would place the Cong foundation some years before 1134.

10

MAP 5

O.S.A. ABBEYS FOUNDED ON NEW SITES

The Augustinian rule required vows of poverty, chastity, obedience, and stability. Its ascetic principles demanded abstention from meat and wine. Its ideal merged contemplation with action, realised in the rule of silence, the practice of manual work, and the *cura animarum*. As with the Cistercians, each new Augustinian foundation consisted of an abbot and twelve canons. Agriculture was necessary for the support of each household and for travellers. Increase in community numbers necessitated the enlargement of their estates and the erection of many agricultural centres which were called courts (*de curtis* or *de curia*) and not granges as within the Cistercian system. The Augustinians accepted ecclesiastical revenues and land cultivated by others; they staffed their hospices, usually built along pilgrimage routes, with lay brothers. Their schools were held in high repute. In 1139–40, Malachy travelled to Rome, where he was appointed papal legate for Ireland. During this journey he visited St. Bernard at Clairvaux and he also visited the abbey of Arrouaise in the diocese of Arras and was impressed by the life of the regular canons there. This abbey had begun as a small settlement of three hermits c. 1090, and had grown into a community by 1097. Richer, the first superior, died in 1121. In the time of his successor, Abbot Gervase (1121–47), the congregation of Arrouaise spread to other places on the continent reaching England by 1133. The Canons of Arrouaise were under the Rule of St. Augustine, with severe observances borrowed from the Cistercians and adopted on the advice of St. Bernard; an abbot of Cîteaux called them Canonico-Cistercians. Under Gervase new houses of the Congregations were usually founded at out-of-the-way places as independent abbeys. Malachy's visit to Arrouaise was in 1140, when Gervase was abbot. Gaultier who was abbot in 1180 states in the introduction to the Cartulary of Arrouaise f. 5, that Malachy inspected and approved the constitutions, books, and church observances, and had them copied so as to take them back to Ireland, where he directed nearly all clerics in episcopal seats and in many other places to adopt and observe them.[19]

Thus before 1137, St. Malachy introduced the Canons Regular of St. Augustine to Ireland, but after 1140, he influenced the adoption of the Arroasian observances at many places in the Northern half of Ireland. The Canons Regular of St. Augustine concentrated on pastoral work while the Canons Regular of St. Augustine of the Arroasian branch dwelt in remote places and were not disposed to undertake the care of collegiate churches or *cura animarum*. By the second half of the fourteenth century, however, most of the Irish houses had dropped both the name and observances of Arrouaise and presumably had become undistinguishable from the general body of Canons Regular. The comprehensive nature of the work of the Canons Regular of St. Augustine and their manifold interests, explain the large number of their foundations in Ireland.

The Cistercians

The Cistercians were monks who followed the Rule of St. Benedict, first written down in the sixth century. Chapter 48 of this rule begins by saying 'idleness is the enemy of the soul, therefore the brothers should be occupied at stated times in manual labour and at other times in sacred reading'. In St. Benedict's monasteries all the monks had what he called 'their appointed tasks'. Some were craftsmen, others worked on the farm or in the garden, for he held that 'a monastery ought if possible to be so constructed that all things necessary such as water, a mill, a garden, a bakery and the various crafts may be contained within it' (chapter 66). The most important occupation in Benedict's scheme was the *Opus Dei*, the Divine Office, chanted at seven periods throughout the day from approximately two hours after midnight, till evening twilight. The hours between each office were taken up with manual work and sacred study (*lectio divina*). Of the two, he seemed to give preference to the former as it followed his legislation for the office and received more coverage than the *lectio*.

St. Benedict's first monastery was at Monte Cassino and it was from this centre that all the great Benedictine monasteries sprang. St. Placid and thirty disciples left Monte Cassino and founded a monastery in Sicily; St. Maur and four companions founded a monastery in Anjou, called St. Maur on the Loire, which became the mother-house of many abbeys. After three centuries Benedictine monasticism showed symptoms of decay. To reform and restore its primitive fervour the Councils of Frankfort (791) and Arles (813) promulgated laws to cut off abuses, principally those that had originated with the adoption of abbots *in commendam*, i.e. laymen or clerics given the honorary title of abbot in order to draw on the abbey's revenues. A further attempt to reform the monasteries took place at the Council of Trosly in AD 909.

It was about that time that William, Duke of Aquitaine, founded the famous abbey of Cluny and placed it under Berno of Baume as first abbot. The latter was succeeded by St. Odo who was styled the 'glory and restorer of the Benedictine Order'. The abbey of Cluny prospered and had three hundred and fourteen monasteries subject to it. One of these daughter-houses of Cluny, Molesme, was governed by a man now known as St. Robert.

After ineffectual attempts to maintain strict observance in his community, he and twenty-one of his more fervent monks resolved to abandon the abbey and establish a regime more in accordance with the original ideals and traditions of the Order. The spot selected for this was Cîteaux in the diocese of Châlons and the province of Burgundy. The monks settled there (21st March 1098), and from its name the new Order which then sprang into existence was called Cistercian. Cîteaux was situated in wasteland, in a difficult physical geographical environment that became the exemplar for a choice of sites from then on in Europe. St. Robert was not destined to complete the great work just begun for before he had well commenced the reform, he received a papal mandate to return to Molesme and resume the government of that house. Two associates, Alberic and Stephen Harding, placed the new order on a firm basis. At first the project at Cîteaux did not prosper, partly because of inadequate manpower. The arrival in 1112 of a young man and thirty followers provided the necessary work force. The new postulant was St. Bernard. His companions were his own brothers, his uncles, and many relatives. Within five years of his entrance, nine new houses of the Order had been founded, the third being Clairvaux of which he was appointed first abbot.

Not only were monasteries becoming numerous but individual ones were increasing in size chiefly by donations. In order to provide a work force to cultivate the extensive abbey lands, Alberic (the second abbot of Cîteaux) introduced a class of monks known as lay brothers. More than a hundred of them might dwell in one house. The expansion of abbey lands meant that some of the cultivated lands were more than a day's walk from the monastery itself. Hence some form of decentralisation was almost inevitable and it took the form of granges, outlying farms with their buildings.

The Cistercians arrived in Ireland in 1142[20] when St. Malachy of Armagh prevailed on his friend St. Bernard to send monks to found an abbey at Mellifont in County Louth. The pattern of development followed that on the continent and by the fifteenth-century suppression of the monasteries under Henry VIII there were thirty-four houses in Ireland.

The differences between the needs of the Canons Regular and the monks were marginal. The Cistercians required isolation for their life of contemplation and study and the possession of land for subsistence. This land was managed, whether for herding or for tillage, mainly by lay brothers. The demands of isolation and the necessity for productive land generally do not go well together. Their skill in land reclamation however usually triumphed over obstacles, so that a common saying was that 'they made the desert bloom'. On the rare occasion when the reclamation failed to meet their needs they changed to a new site. They differed from the Canons Regular in that their constitutions made them depend entirely on land for subsistence. The Canons could receive alms and an income from ecclesiastical benefices; but this was forbidden to the Cistercians.

MAP 6

CIST. ABBEYS FOUNDED ON NEW SITES.
FOR DETAILS SEE TABLE 6, P. 124.

THE DISTRIBUTION OF MEDIEVAL AUGUSTINIAN
AND CISTERCIAN ABBEYS

'Do you in the meantime with the wisdom given you by
the Lord, look for and prepare a site similar to what you
have seen here, far removed from the turmoil of the
world.'

Bernard, Letter 383.

With the coming to Ireland of the great continental
orders of monks and canons, the native Irish became acquainted for the first time with that large building complex that we call a medieval abbey, a monastery on a scale
vastly exceeding anything hitherto seen in the country.
The buildings were erected on sites judged to be suitable.

Since one of the aims of this study is to explain why some of those abbeys prospered more than others, it is logical to attempt a physical classification which both simplifies and summarises possibilities for economic development. Every site has been examined both cartographically and in the field, and the results of the field work investigation are shown in Appendix A, p. 99.

It is possible to divide the sites into two main types, namely, those which favoured development and those in which growth was unlikely. Abbeys were normally sited where solid rock lay just below the surface and near to a supply of building stone. They were usually found in close proximity to a water supply although at four sites examined in this work, windmills were used. Possession of fertile lands and a nodal position both favoured growth; restricted sites generally inhibited it. However suitable siting alone was not a guarantee of the development of abbeys.

There are two things to be considered: (a) the general distribution of monastic sites; and (b) the physical classification of sites.

(A) GENERAL DISTRIBUTION

One of the controlling factors in the location of medieval monastic sites was the already existing network of Celtic sites (MAP 7). This density was not followed by an equal distribution of medieval abbeys. The Orders from the continent occupied only seventy of the one hundred ninety-seven recorded[21] Celtic sites. The superimposition of Map 1 on Map 7, however, shows a similar pattern of occupation. Therefore it is reasonable to assume that the same locating factors were operative in these cases. For instance Map 7 indicates large areas with no abbeys. These are mainly mountainous districts and areas of bogland. The altitudes of the forementioned Celtic sites have been examined; forty-nine of them were under 200 ft. above sea level, from which it may be concluded that Celtic founders tended to occupy lowlands (SEE TABLE 7).

MAP 7

THE DISTRIBUTION OF CELTIC MONASTIC SITES

Areas of lowland bog, however, were avoided and Map 8 shows there were four main areas of lowland bog: (1) on both banks of the River Shannon around Lough Ree where it has been estimated to cover 176,000 acres; (2) between the Westmeath Uplands and the Shannon (3) an area extending from King's county to north-west Kildare and (4) from Banagher and Athlone eastwards to the Liffey. If Map 1 showing the distribution of medieval abbeys is superimposed on Map 8 showing the distribution of bogland, one sees that both Augustinians and Cistercians avoided these areas.

18

MAP 8
MAP OF THE DISTRIBUTION OF BOGLAND

Siting in relation to population distribution

Because of the nature of the Augustinian Order the majority of the abbeys were most likely to have been established in heavily populated areas. On the whole the distribution of medieval abbeys tends to be similar to that of population (SEE MAP 9). The pattern of settlement in medieval Ireland as shown by the distribution of raths[22] is generally accepted as indicative of the distribution of population in Celtic and early Medieval Ireland.

STONE   BUILT   RATH

Equivalent to a 30 acre farm (12 hectares). In other areas the raths were of mud wall type.

A RATH

However, two problems emerge. Whereas the lack of raths in mountainous areas is indicative of a lack of settlement in the Celtic era, there is a similar paucity in the early medieval period. This paucity in the extreme northeast is less easy to explain. In east and central Ireland it appears, according to McCourt,[23] that many raths had been destroyed by the Normans and that the present distribution is only a relic of a larger one. In the extreme northeast the lack of raths has been attributed not so much to their removal as to alternative forms of contemporary settlement. Watson,[24] basing his evidence on Pope Nicholas' taxation of 1306 for Antrim, agrees with this idea and Proudfoot has similar findings for County Down.

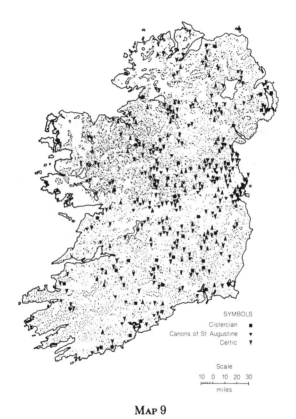

MAP 9

THE MAP (AFTER D. MCCOURT) OF THE DISTRIBUTION OF MONASTIC SITES
SUPERIMPOSED ON THE MAP OF THE RATHS
(EACH DOT REPRESENTS A RATH)

The Celtic distribution of monasteries is seen under two
forms (a) eremetical structures on islands and the mountains of the west, on the islands in the Shannon lakes of Al-
len, Ree and Derg; and (b) large and wealthy monasteries
such as Kells and Clonard. Map 9, the superimposition of
Map 7, showing the distribution of Celtic monasteries,
upon a map showing the distribution of raths reveals that
although some Celtic monasteries were in isolated areas
the larger ones followed the distribution of population.
However, in the east and central Ireland, only a few Celtic

monasteries are found in areas where there are not many raths. According to O Corrain, 'by 800 A.D. many monasteries had developed into monastic towns with populations large by medieval standards.'[25] Durrow for example, lost two hundred men in a battle with Clonmacnoise in 764 and if there is any reality behind that number it argues for a population of between fifteen hundred and two thousand people[26]. An account of an attack on Kells in 951, less than a century and a half after foundation, states that three thousand persons or more were captured and that a large booty of goods, horses, gold and silver were taken. Even if these figures mean simply large numbers, considerable wealth and population are implied[27]. By the ninth century there were monastic towns with streets of wooden houses, types of building that were contemporary with the rath. In 1090 about one hundred houses were burned in the city of Armagh. Two years later its rath and two streets were burned, followed by a further three streets in 1172. Other entries indicate well-known divisions of the city. Lastly, in 1166 a major fire took place there resulting in the burning of many areas including several churches and buildings and some four or five streets.[28] The lack of raths in east and central Ireland (as shown on Map 9) may indicate that they were replaced by streets as in a 'monastic city' or that they were obliterated by the Normans.

The superimposition of the map of the distribution of medieval abbeys (Map 1) on McCourt's map of the distribution of raths shows that the distribution of raths was more even than was that of medieval monasteries (Map 9). There is a remarkable concentration of medieval abbeys in east and central Ireland corresponding to areas of dense population. J.H. Andrews in *The Course of Irish History* says:

> In the east, the land is generally kinder, and if we draw one line from Lough Owel to Dundalk and another to meet the coast just south of Dublin we have marked off the heart of this eastern zone.

He is speaking of the Eastern Triangle,

> a part of Ireland which receives less rain, and contains less
> bog and mountain than any other compact area of similar
> size[29]... The eastern triangle is the geographical nucleus
> from which men have seen their best chance of comman-
> ding the whole country.[30]

In this area the Augustinians had thirteen and the Cistercians three foundations.

SITING IN RELATION TO COMMUNICATIONS: ROADS — RIVERS

Map 10 compiled by McLochlainn[31] in 1940, shows the
ancient roads of Ireland, its topographical features, typ-
onomy, river crossings, scenes of battles fought between
AD 450 and 1000, ancient royal seats, journey routes based
on early literature (432–942), with certain nodal points. It
reveals that these were recognised routes of long standing.
On these roads forty-two places are named, thirty of which
subsequently turn up as Augustinian and ten as Cistercian
locations, which indicates that the Augustinians and Cistercians chose places already accessible by public routeway, (SEE TABLE 8, P. 126). Their experience in European
monasteries had showed that this was vital for a successful
economy. However, the most revealing fact about this
map is that there are no roads indicated for county Kerry,
only one for Cork, one for Waterford in the south-east,
and none for Co. Fermanagh. This is due to the relief of
the land. In Cork and Kerry, the east-west trend of the
mountain ranges made a north to south traverse difficult.

High bare or bog-encumbered country intervenes between the long valleys opening to the Atlantic, and between the Lee and Blackwater which flow eastwards to
the sea. Moorland with wide tracts of peat extend from the
Shannon estuary southwards, rising to 1341 ft. in the Mullaghareirk Mountains and so separating the lowland

draining westward to Dingle Bay and Tralee Bay from the plain of the Upper Blackwater. The most practicable route from east to west passes up the Blackwater valley between the Mullaghareirk Mountains and the Derry-nasaggart via Millstreet and Rathmore to Killarney. There is, however, no crossing of this highland boundary at a lower elevation than 900 ft.

The east-west barrier trend is continued towards the east in the Knockmealdowns, Monavullagh and Comeragh Mountains. One road, as shown on Map 10 leads from the Central Plain to Waterford, and follows the Barrow valley between the Castlecomer Plateau and the Slieve Ardagh Hills, then follows a gap between Mount Brandon and the Blackstairs. In early days this was thickly forested and the district between Slieve Margy and Mount Brandon was known as the Bealach Gabhran (Pass of Gowran). Bowen recognises the distribution of seventh and eighth century Celtic monasteries as being mainly to the north of the 'South Ireland End Moraine'[32] though obviously the real obstacle to settlement south of this was the forementioned east-west ranges that run parallel to the moraine.

In Co. Fermanagh the main obstacle to communications from the Central Plain was the Erne river basin with its two lakes, Upper and Lower Lough Erne. The swamp and bog characteristic of the country around Upper Lough Erne, and the forests of Lower Lough Erne, proved as effective obstacle to access to the west coast for centuries.

The map of Medieval Augustinian and Cistercian abbeys, (Map 1), shows that their siting was not governed by the considerations which influenced native Irish monks; many are found on the southern rivers, (See Map 11) in contrast to the Celtic pattern (Map 7).

24

ROADWAYS IN ANCIENT IRELAND

MAP 10
(AFTER McLOCHLAIN)

MAP 11

☐ ◇ ABBEY DEPENDENT ON RIVER COMMUNICATIONS:
MAINLY SOUTH OF THE GREAT TERMINAL MORAINE
BOWEN'S OBERSERVATION BEING THAT THE 7TH & 8TH C.
CELTIC MONASTERIES LAY TO THE NORTH OF THIS.

Problems of classifications of the physical sites of medieval abbeys

It is possible to divide the sites of medieval abbeys into four main categories: eighty-one were in valley sites, nineteen on 'islands' surrounded by water or bog, 10 on drumlins and 20 on sites which are here termed 'miscellaneous'. (Table 9 and Table 10, pp. 127–128). This classification poses problems, firstly because it is difficult to assign some abbeys to a particular category because of their intermediate position, and secondly because no category necessarily completely excludes another. For example, Clonmacnoise could fall into more than one classification: it is both near to the River Shannon and in its valley, but it was sited on an esker, which formed the base of an important routeway to Clonmacnoise (see Illustrations 1 and 2). The valley at this point is ill-defined and the siting was clearly dominated by the esker which provided both dry land above the surrounding bogs and a crossing point. Other abbeys of this type—Ballyboggan, Durrow, Great Connell and Caher, all in the vicinity of eskers—are however included in the category of valley bottom sitings because they are found at the foot of the eskers on the valley floor, the road skirting the foot of the esker rather than being actually on it, as at Clonmacnoise. Even with this a third variation occurs at Corbally, where the abbey is at the foot of an esker, with no routeway crossing the top or skirting the bottom, and only a small stream running northwards about one thousand yards to the east of the site, so rather than call this a valley bottom siting it has been termed 'miscellaneous' (See Map 12).

Problems of classification also arise with the category 'islands in lake, sea or bog'. Killah Abbey is 1672 feet from the River Maine and Clonfert Abbey is 2,211 feet from the River Suck. Both seem to be river valley sitings. But the river flows through extensive bogs and the only suitable sitings are on islands of glacial material which rise above bog level. Hence the sites are more sensibly described as island ones rather than river valley sites.

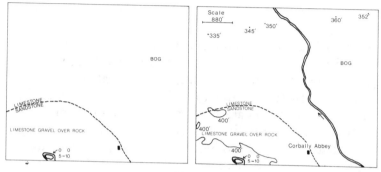

MAP 12

Occasionally an abbey might fall into three categories, such as Inch Abbey, which is situated on the slope of a gentle drumlin on the left bank of the Quoile estuary, and one hundred yards from the sea. Although it bears the characteristics of the first three categories its proximity to tidal water suggests that it be classified with the miscellaneous sitings of category four.

Problems arise with the term coastal, and how to define it. A coastal site could theoretically be at a distance of ten miles from the sea or could be visible from the sea or adjacent to tidal water. Often there is an abbey in a valley site within ten miles of the sea, giving two options for classification. In this paper the term coastal site includes those within ten miles of the sea provided the area has no river, as at Maure Abbey and Grey Abbey, proximity to the sea being the overriding consideration.

Some abbeys could not be included in the first three categories so they have been placed under the heading miscellaneous. The term miscellaneous is used to accommodate other peculiar abbey sites such as Kilcooley on a mountain slope (400 ft.), Roscommon on a ridge, Kilmacduagh surrounded by turloughs and Kilshanny on a dissected kame.

River Valleys	Islands in Lake, Sea, Bog	Drumlins	Miscellaneous
81	19	10	20

Following such a classification Augustinian and Cistercian abbeys were sited as follows:

	Group 1	Group 2	Group 3	Group 4
	River Valleys	Islands in Lake, Sea, Bog	Drumlins	Miscellaneous
Augustinians	56	18	9	13
Cistercians	25	1	1	7

Each group will be examined in turn.

GROUP 1: RIVER VALLEY SITINGS

Map 13 and Tables 11–16 (p. 129–133) show that the majority of Augustinian and Cistercian abbeys were sited in river valleys.

28

MAP 13

PHYSICAL CLASSIFICATION OF MONASTIC SITES

Of the thirty-nine new sites chosen by the Augustinians twenty-nine were in river valleys, and of the twenty-one chosen by the Cistercians seventeen were similarly located. The term river valley denotes a general rather than a specific situation. Abbeys in river valleys however drew from this type of location certain advantages such as accessibility, availability of water for domestic needs and a power supply, possibilities for fishing and the prospect of water meadows. The precise siting of abbeys within a valley was determined not only by a potentially greater facility for using the water at any given point, but also by other considerations such as the presence of a solid foundation on which to build, a feature by no means ubiquitous in river valleys. Generally abbeys were built as near to water as possible on a solid foundation which was necessarily above flood level. Hence low river terraces where rock was near the surface were especially favoured, nevertheless there was a hierarchy of siting values, namely:

A – Water Requirements;   B – Solid foundations;
C – Building stone;   D – Human factors.

A – Water Requirements

All medieval abbeys needed water for two purposes (1) for domestic supply and (2) for power.

(1) Siting in relation to water requirements for domestic purposes:

A good domestic water supply was essential to a medieval abbey. Monasteries were spacious buildings planned to accommodate large and active communities. The abbey's life line was the abbey stream. This was usually an artificial water course cut from some nearby stream for the benefit of the monastery alone. Both Augustinian and Cistercian abbeys were built to a standard plan which was based on the assumption that an artificial water course could be engineered, passing first of all along the southern side of the claustral complex and if possible flowing from west to east, so as to pass the refectory and kitchen before reaching the rear dorter at the end of the monks' house. Therefore in order to accommodate the standard plan, the engineering of the Great Sewer and the water conduits demanded that the site should have a north west to south east slope. This resulted in fifty-one out of fifty-six Augustinian and eighteen out of twenty-five Cistercian abbeys being sited on the right banks of rivers. However, this was only a general consideration, for most of the right banks would fulfill this desideratum.

Ancillary to the advantage of the site having a north west to south east slope was the ease with which the abbey stream could be carried through the offices of the abbey in buried conduits to flush and well up in those parts of the abbey where it was needed, and then, having fulfilled its appointed task, to return to the river.

(2) *Siting in relation to water requirements for power*:

All medieval abbeys required either water or wind.[33] Mills were always located outside the abbey precincts, even at some distance from the abbey. A table of distance from the perimeter wall of the abbey to the nearest point on the millstream was drawn up in relation to new sites only, as above. Some problems arose in cases where there is no archaeological or hydrological evidence for millstreams, but evidence available indicates the following for Augustinians:

(CANONS) AUGUSTINIANS

NAME OF ABBEY	DISTANCE TO MILLSTREAM
Abbeyderg	NE
Athassel	704'
Abbeygormacan	NE
Ballintober	NE
Ballybeg	NE
Ballyboggan	NE
Ballymore	NE
Bridgetown	NE
Caher	88'
Clare	NE
Down	264'
Dublin All Saints	NE
Dublin St. Thomas	NE
Glendalough (St. Saviours')	NE
Great Connell	352'
Kells (M)	NE
Kells (O)	NE
Kilkenny	NE
Mullingar	88'
Naas	1200'
Newtown Trim	880'
Rathkeale	NE
St. Catherine's Dublin	NE
St. Wolstan's C.	NE
Tuam	3000'

TABLE 17
(CANONS) AUGUSTINIANS

and for Cistercians:

(CANONS) CISTERCIANS

NAME OF ABBEY	DISTANCE TO MILLSTREAM
Abbeyknockmoy	800'
Abbeyleix	NE
Abbeyshrule	100'
Abington	264'
Assaroe	NE
Baltinglass	704'
Bective	704'
Boyle	2200'
Dunbrody	NE
Fermoy	NE
Graiguenamanagh	350'
Inishlounaght	704'
Kilbeggan	1320'
Macosquin	NE
Mellifont	1056'
Tintern	4400'
Tracton	352'

TABLE 18

CISTERCIANS

KEY FOR TABLES 17, 18, 21, 22

N   = nearer to river than to millstream
S   = same distance to river as to millstream
NE = no evidence
O   = Abbey is nearer to the millstream than to the river

32

When these tables have been compared with those of distance to domestic water supply

(Canons) Augustinians

Name of Abbey	Distance in feet from domestic water supply
Bridgetown	15'
Newtown Trim	30'
Ballyboggan	45'
Kells (O)	45'
Athassel	60'
Abbeygormacan	80'
Caher	176'
Dublin All Saints	176'
Ballybeg	200'
Mullingar	440'
Ballintober	704'
Kilkenny	704'
Great Connell	1144'
Rathkeale	2640'
Tuam	3000'
Kells (M)	4400'

TABLE 19

Canons Regular of St. Augustine

CISTERCIANS

NAME OF ABBEY	DISTANCE IN FEET FROM DOMESTIC WATER SUPPLY
Assaroe	20'
Fermoy	50'
Kilbeggan	50'
Graiguenamanagh	60'
Abbeyleix	75'
Mellifont	80'
Boyle	88'
Abbeyshrule	100'
Tintern	120'
Abbeyknockmoy	150'
Tracton	176'
Inishlounaght	240'
Abington	264'
Bective	300'
Dunbrody	528'

TABLE 20

CISTERCIANS

the summary evidence is that at only two Augustinian sites (Great Connell and Mullingar) was the millstream within the abbey complex and nearer to the abbey than to the river. For Cistercian sites a similar exercise was undertaken and in no case was the site nearer to its power supply than to its domestic supply; therefore, as far as precise siting was concerned, the evidence pointed to greater proximity to domestic supply. However, as Tables 21 and 22 show,

AUGUSTINIANS

NAME OF ABBEY	DISTANCE TO MILLSTREAM IN FEET	DISTANCE TO RIVER IN FEET	
Abbeyderg	—	300'	NE
Athassel	176	60'	N
Abbeygormacan	—	60'	NE
Ballintober	—	704'	NE
Ballybeg	—	200'	NE
Ballyboggan	—	45'	N
Ballymore	—	—	NE
Bridgetown	—	15'	N
Caher	88'	176'	N
Clare	—	80'	N
Down	264'	100'	N
Dublin All Saints	—	176'	N
Dublin St. Thomas	—	—	
St. Sav. Glendal.	—	—	NE
Great Connell	352'	1144'	O
Kells (M)	—	4400'	NE
Kells (O)	880'	45'	N
Kilkenny	—	704'	NE
Mullingar	88'	440'	O
Naas	1200'	—	NE
Newtown Trim	880'	30'	N
Rathkeale	—	2640'	NE
St. Cath. Dublin	—	—	
St. Wolstans Dublin	—	—	
Tuam	3000'	3000'	S

TABLE 21

SUMMARY:

10 = NE
9 = N
1 = S
2 = O

NAME OF ABBEY	DISTANCE TO MILLSTREAM IN FEET	DISTANCE TO RIVER IN FEET	
Abbeyknockmoy	800'	150'	N
Abbeyleix	—	75'	—
Abbeyshrule	100'	100'	S
Abington	264'	264'	S
Assaroe	—	20'	
Baltinglass	704'	264'	N
Bective	704'	300'	N
Boyle	2200'	88'	
Dunbrody	—	528'	N
Fermoy	—	50'	
Graiguenamanagh	350'	60'	
Inishlounaght	704'	240'	N
Kilbeggan	1320'	50'	N
Macosquin	—	—	N
Mellifont	1056'	80'	N
Tintern	4400'	120'	N
Tracton	352'	176'	N

TABLE 22

the distance variation was not all that extensive, and since the functions were complementary domestic supply and power requirements may be discussed simultaneously herewith.

There are two types of water power situation:

Type (a) facilities offered by a geomorphological situation in a major river valley for mill race construction namely: (i) alluvium that could be cut through; (ii) meander loops; (iii) riffles.

Type (b) a tributary stream with a relatively steep gradient. Hence there were two types of abbeys (i) those within 300 feet of a river that had no mill race (ii) those with mill races on the rivers.

Type (a)

Mill races were variable in size and in the ways in which they were constructed. The monasteries were clearly endowed with enough labour and skill to construct both wide and lengthy mill races. The two most outstanding examples were Athassel and Great Connell. At Athassel the abbey was sited on an alluvial flat within a meander loop of over one mile amplitude (See Map 14A)

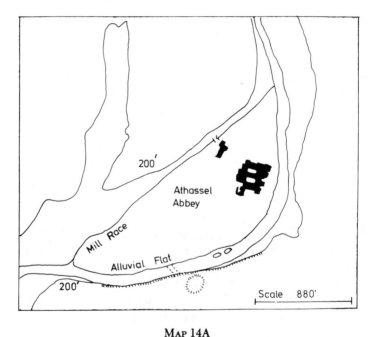

Map 14A

Athassel Abbey Co. Tipperary

and a NE-SW down gradient as shown

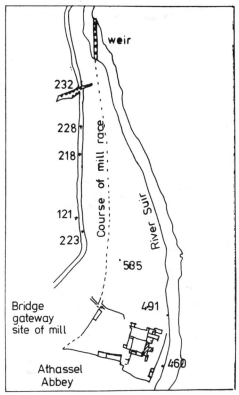

MAP 14B
ATHASSEL ABBEY CO. TIPPERARY

with rock outcrops at both of its extremities. The Augustinians cut a mill race across the loop, an operation requiring very extensive excavation lengthwise and breadthwise, for the complete mill race required the building of a mill bridge over forty feet wide to span it (SEE ILLUSTRATIONS 3 AND 4).

Nevertheless the abbey buildings were nearer to the river than the mill race was. (SEE MAPS 14A AND PLAN 1) which indicate part of the Great Drain as a return effluent to the River Suir.

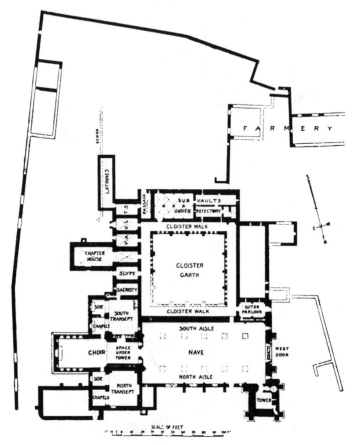

PLAN 1

PLAN OF ATHASSEL PRIORY

Great Connell Abbey cut a mill race over a mile long, through low terrace material, as the River Liffey follows a very meandering course. Reference to the geological map on which the Ordnance Survey map has been superimposed shows that this mill race has been cut in river alluvium along the lower limit of a limestone gravel esker (SEE MAP 15).

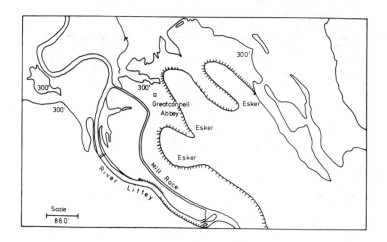

MAP 15
GREAT CONNELL ABBEY CO. KILDARE

In this instance the abbey was over a quarter of a mile from the river and the domestic water supply may have been led from the millstream itself.

Riffles in the major river were the most characteristic of the water power situation. Of fourteen Cistercian abbeys, all situated on major rivers, eight fall into this category and of the twenty-five abbeys belonging to the Augustinians, twelve belong to this type. (SEE TABLE 10 P. 128 AND TABLE 9 P. 127.) A good example is Holy Cross Abbey, Co. Tipperary, situated on a river terrace (300 feet) where the islands in the river facilitated a build up of water in a restricted channel from which a small cut was made to allow the water to pass through the mill wheel and a small tail race for the return of the water to the Suir, (SEE ILLUSTRATIONS 5 AND 6). The domestic supply was obtained from a well sunk in the bank of the river and from this conduits were led through the domestic buildings facilitated by the north to south slope of the ground from 300 feet to 287 feet (at mill bridge).

40

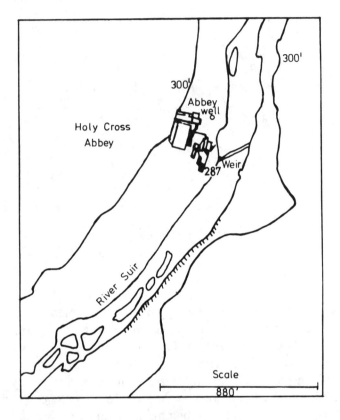

MAP 16

HOLY CROSS ABBEY CO. TIPPERARY

Kells Abbey, Co. Kilkenny, situated on the right bank of the King's River, lies in an amphitheatre-like hollow with an incline of over 200 feet (SEE MAP 17 AND ILLUSTRATIONS 9 AND 10—NOTE 210 FEET CONTOUR).

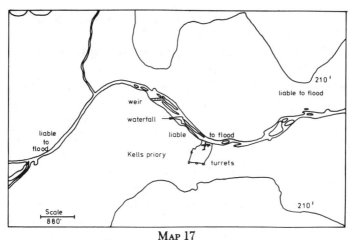

MAP 17
KELLS PRIORY CO. KILKENNY

As at Holy Cross there are many point bars in the river over the best part of a mile; these were used for mill construction. Reference to Plan 2 shows the dispostion of the buildings within the precinct which covers five acres.

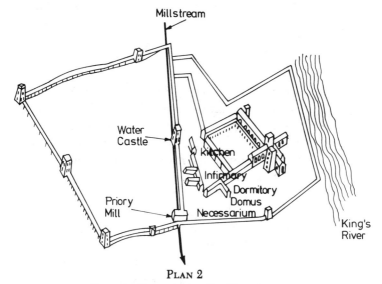

PLAN 2
PLAN OF KELLS ABBEY CO. KILKENNY.
(COURTESY OF THE BOARD OF WORKS DUBLIN)

The kitchen, the infirmary and the Domus Necessarium were external to the cloister. A stream was cut from the King's river to flow from north west to south east. It ran along a well marked course on the Burgess Court side of the central dividing wall between the two courts, making its entry by way of a wide pointed archway. It passed beneath the bridge of the Great Gateway and by way of a vaulted passage under the first floor unit of the water castle (water tower). This was a conduit house, twenty feet square (PLAN 2). Inside this conduit house there was a column to give a head of pressure and from it water was distributed to various important points throughout the domestic offices mentioned above. The millstream made its exit through a double archway and passing by the abbey mill made its exit from the latter through a double archway in the east wall of the Burgess Court and then returned to the river. The Augustinians used a conduit drawn from the millstream to service the house as well as the abbey mill. Monasternenagh, Co. Limerick, situated on a peneplane of limestone was another site with excellent facilities for water exploitation due to the presence of riffles in the Camoge River.

Type (b)

The most desirable situation for water exploitation was a point at which a small tributary flowed down a fairly steep slope into a major valley. This provided the dual requirements of sufficient velocity without too great a volume and provided the optimum siting requirements in relation to water power. Such locations were met with at five large important Cistercian sites: Mellifont, Assaroe, Monasternenagh, Inishlounaght, and Graiguenamanagh; and at eleven Augustinian sites: Bridgetown, Ferns, Abbeydown, Inistioge, Kells (Co. Antrim), Kells (Co. Meath), Killeigh, Rathkeale, Rattoo, Cong and Caher (MAP 19). Reference to Map 18 and Illustration 11 shows the ideal conditions for water power, at Inistioge, Co. Kilkenny.

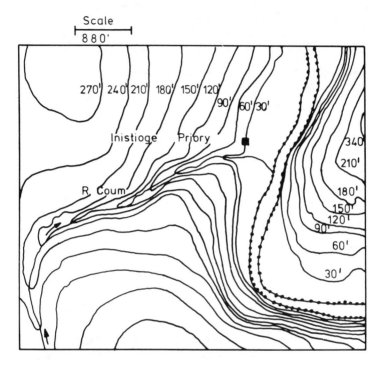

MAP 18

INISTIOGE PRIORY CO. KILKENNY

The main river, the Nore, is flowing through a broad flat bottomed valley, the abbey is sited beyond the inundation line on the right bank where a tributary, the River Coum but today called the Mill Stream, descends through a defile to reach the main river. This abbey is sited on the solid rock of slates and grits which can be seen exposed in the valley sides. Another ideal siting for water power was found at Caher, Co. Tipperary (MAP 19), where the abbey was sited on the right bank of the River Suir on an outcrop of carboniferous limestone.

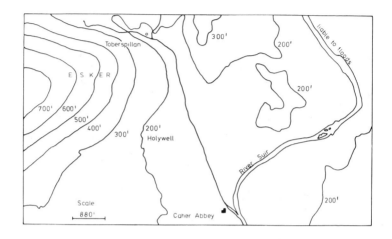

MAP 19
CAHER ABBEY CO. TIPPERARY

To the west there is a silver sand and gravel esker. A stream runs from a spring in the gravel esker and the point at which this stream enters the River Suir became the precise siting of the abbey, the esker acting as an aquifer for the abbey mill stream.

Bridgetown Abbey, Co. Cork, is situated on an outcrop of carboniferous limestone in the incised Blackwater Valley (SEE MAP 20).

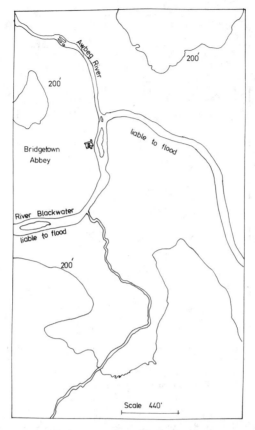

MAP 20
BRIDGETOWN ABBEY CO. CORK

As shown on the map the abbey is sited where there is a
marked change in the direction of the River Blackwater
from east to northwards and then eastwards again three
hundred feet from its confluence with the Awbeg. Reference to the ground plan of this abbey shows that it departs
from the standard plan, but nevertheless sites the Great
Kitchen within fifteen feet of the river. Plan 3 (P. 46) shows
the vaulted passage or conduit leading the water from the
river through the domestic offices.

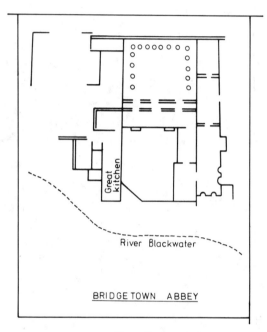

Great kitchen

River Blackwater

BRIDGETOWN ABBEY

PLAN 3
BRIDGETOWN ABBEY CO. CORK

There was the additional advantage at the site for power because of point bars and riffles in the River Blackwater in the vicinity of the abbey.

At Inishlounaght Abbey, Co. Tipperary, situated on the left bank of the Suir, a side stream had to be more or less contrived. The abbey was sited eighty yards from the left bank of the Suir beyond the inundation line. On this left bank there is a lateral moraine over one hundred feet high, to the north of which is a stream originating in St. Patrick's Well, and through this moraine the Cistercians cut an artificial channel, to-day called the Marlfield Stream, to drive their mill, the slope of the moraine providing the swift gradient for power, (MAP 21).

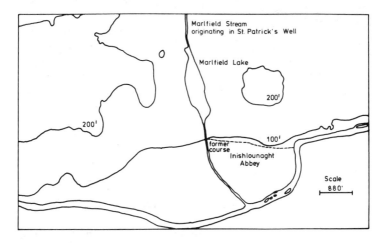

MAP 21

INISHLOUNAGHT ABBEY CO. TIPPERARY

Twenty Augustinian and six Cistercian abbeys were sited along minor streams, approximately ten feet wide, of any order other than a first order stream. In such streams there were no point bars but the narrow channel of the stream provided sufficient volume to drive wheels. Some of these minor streams so meandered, however, that a mill race had to be cut to accelerate the flow; for example, at Mellifont Abbey, Co. Louth, a mill race 2,640 feet long was cut to avoid the meander loops of the Mattock River.

Glendalough, Co. Wicklow, is a typical U-shaped valley. There are rock exposures of schists on both sides of the valley, especially along the southern shore of the Upper Lake. The valley floor is occupied by two lakes (SEE MAP 22 AND ILLUSTRATION 12).

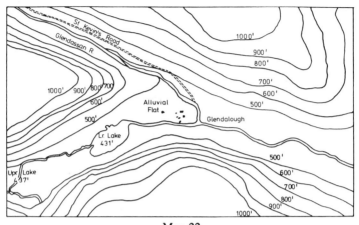

MAP 22
GLENDALOUGH ABBEY CO. WICKLOW

Between these there is an alluvial flat and at the mouth of
the Glendassan River (SEE MAP 22) an accumulation of bedded sand and gravel which stands about twenty feet above
it to about four hundred and sixty feet, where the monastic remains of the Seven Churches of St. Kevin's Monastery are sited. This is a fan formation which is the same as
in some Welsh Celtic sites in glaciated valleys. The Celtic
Monastery was founded by St. Kevin in the sixth century
on a site between the two lakes. Disciples flocked to him in
what was at first his hermitage beside the Upper Lake and
there were soon several cells under his rule. 'On the northern shore of the lake his dwelling was a hollow tree, on the
southern shore he dwelt in a narrow cave to which there
was no access except by boat, for a perpendicular rock of
great height overhangs it from above',[34] an Old Life of the
Saint informs us. This abbey survived as a Celtic site into
the twelfth century, a long list of abbots is recorded and
St. Laurence O'Toole, abbot from 1153 to 1162, changed
the rule to that of the Canons Regular of St. Augustine.
Half a mile southeast of the Celtic site, St. Laurence
founded another monastery for the Augustinians called St.
Saviour's Priory, where he and a few monks resided.

B - Solid Foundations

River systems in Ireland are so constituted that rocks are often exposed in them or in the valleys alongside them. In such places, the abbeys were enabled to avoid drift and this was of prime importance with regard to the siting of an abbey. Abbey buildings were massive stone structures, so that the foremost consideration influencing the choice of site would be its practical geology. Unless the foundations were carried down to actual rock, a trench had to be dug out and filled to a variable depth to form a footing of somewhat greater breadth than the wall to be raised upon it. Furthermore, in order to adjust the courses of the infill when there were slight variations in the depth of the foundations, the medieval builders used slates to even off the courses. Evidence of this is seen in the excavations of Mellifont Abbey (See Map 24) and at Kells Abbey (Illustration 15). Solid foundations were preferable. Therefore it is not surprising to find abbeys sited on rock outcrops in valleys (Table 23, p. 51). Out of one hundred and thirty monastic sites only eleven were on limestone drift (See Map 23 and Appendix B, p. 111).

Intimately connected with this type of rock is its disposition, the cardinal rule to be followed by both the Augustinians and the Cistercians, was that the chancel end of the church should be placed due east and that the cloisters should be on the south side. Furthermore, there was a tendency for the medieval builder to so plan the building that the long axis of the church ran parallel with the strike of the rocks. This tendency was shown in the Cistercian abbeys of Tintern, Hore, Holy Cross, Abbeyshrule, Knockmoy, Tracton, Abbeymahon, and Boyle, and in the Augustinian abbeys at Newtown-Trim, Caher, Athassel, Innisfallen, Inistioge, Bridgetown, Gill, and Celbridge. Field work investigation shows that at fifty-six sites, thirty-seven of which were at valley bottom, there were

Scale 10 0 10 20 30
miles

Abbeys in the vicinity of which there are rock exposures.

map 10

Map 23
ABBEYS IN THE VICINITY OF WHICH THERE ARE ROCK EXPOSURES

ABBEYS IN THE VICINITY OF WHICH THERE WERE ROCK EXPOSURES

AUGUSTINIANS	CISTERCIANS
Abbeyderg	Abbeylara
Aghmacart	Abbeyshrule
Athassel	Abington
Aughrim	Abbeymahon
Aughris	Abbeystrowry
Ballinskelligs	Baltinglass
Ballintober	Boyle
Ballybeg	Corcomroe
Ballysadare	Cashel
Bridgetown	Graiguenamanagh
Cahir	Holy Cross
Clare	Inishlounahgt
Cong	Kilcooley
Errew	Knockmoy
Ferns	Mellifont
Fertagh	Middleton
Gill	Newry
Holmpatrick	Tintern
Inistioge	Tracton
Innisfallen	
Kells (K)	
Kells (M)	
Killagh	
Killeigh	
Kilmacduagh	
Lisgoole	
Mayo	
Mohill	
Monasternenagh	
Mothel	
Navan	
Newtown Trim	
Roscommon	
St. Wolstans	
Trim	
Tristernagh	
Wexford	

TABLE 23

rock exposures (SEE MAP 23.) The geology of the sites is shown in Appendix B, p. 111. Unfortunately excavation work on some of these medieval abbey sites has just begun. Holy Cross Abbey which has been excavated and photographed shows the carboniferous limestone bed on which the abbey was raised (ILLUSTRATION 16.)

Mellifont Abbey, Co. Louth, is sited on the left bank of the River Mattock (MAP 24). The underlying rock, which is exposed on the scarps of the valley, is composed of silurian slates and grits, and in the lower part of the valley a thin deposit of sand and gravel covers the rock. Over this there is a thickness of several feet of stiff yellow glacial drift, relatively free from stones, which forms the subsoil of the valley floor. In 1959 Mellifont Abbey was excavated and the following section drawings have been produced from that work[35] (ILLUSTRATIONS 13 AND 14). Excavation of the church revealed that from about half-way along the length of the church the underlying bedrock dips steeply towards the River Mattock. The twelfth century builders brought the walls of the church down to the bedrock and inserted a crypt under the west end of the nave, thereby replacing the clay sub-soil by the stronger foundation. 'A western crypt as described above is unusual and in the Mellifont crypt the distance from the church floor to the crypt floor level was not quite seven feet overall'[36] so human comfort was not a consideration in building it. Its primary purpose was probably structural, especially for the provision of a firm basis on the solid rock for the nave arcades.

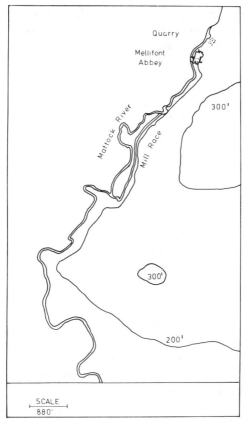

MAP 24
MELLIFONT ABBEY CO. LOUTH

C – Building Stone

Complementary to rock outcrops was the possibility of obtaining good quality building stone *in situ* at a desirable siting place in a river valley bottom. This enhances the quality of the site but was only a secondary factor in determining the precise siting of abbeys. The romanesque traditional style of early abbeys demanded a considerable amount of material even for a comparatively modest building, but when a work of first magnitude such as Jerpoint or Cong was proposed with wall thickness of four feet, then the total material requirements became enormous. The tendency therefore was to use local building stone, rather than bring stone from a distance. On the other hand, if stone had to be brought from a distance, then in order to avoid the great expense and delay involved in land carriage, it was brought down the river in question to the proposed abbey site.

The universally recognised average strength of the principal rocks is in the following order: slate, basalt, limestone, granite, sandstone, but field work investigation shows that the Augustinian and Cistercian abbeys were mainly sited on the limestone rocks. This tendency is unquestionably weighted by the geological structure of Ireland and the distribution of limestone throughout the country. Within the limestone group, the primary limestones and the compact hard calp are the strongest and the light dove coloured fossiliferous the weakest, but as Appendix B, p. 111 shows, although there was a wide range of choice, both orders were inclined towards the primary limestones, and building stone was mainly that of the local rocks in the vicinity of the proposed site. At some sites the actual location of the quarries from which the building stones was obtained is known. At Mellifont the quarry that supplied the main building material lay five hundred and twenty-eight feet north of the site. In the land donation of Holy Cross, a cliff called Sgearda is mentioned in its charter.[37] The modern six inch Ordnance Survey 1840 map indicates Poll na Sgearda, the cliff quarry from which the monks obtained limestone for their buildings. This siting with such a convenient stone was probably more by accident than by design. However, it proved to be an excellent quality stone both for receiving finely wrought carving and for its durability, for the mouldings of the oldest part are still fresh and sharp on the edges and even the marks of the tools are still preserved. It was capable of being punched, chiselled, tooled and sparrow-pecked.

On the north side of Boyle Abbey, (See Map 25 and Illustration 17), at a place called John's Hole, is the quarry from which the monks of Boyle obtained a good sandstone for their abbey.

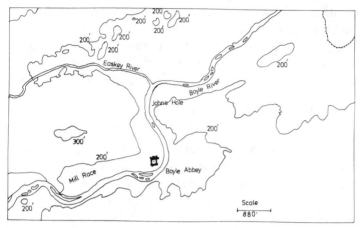

MAP 25
BOYLE ABBEY CO. ROSCOMMON

In its ruins one finds excellent work of every kind from common plain dressed stone to carved mouldings and ornaments, and its lofty arches display great skill in construction. The stone has well resisted exposure to weather, some of the marks of the tools being still visible. From the same quarry excellent flags with a smooth natural face could be procured. These are of large size from five inches to six inches thick, five feet to seven feet long and three feet wide. Limestone for mortar was obtained from Cogan's Field Quarry, one mile distant, and pit sand was procurable from a half mile to two miles from the abbey site.

Wicklow is the only county in Ireland which does not contain limestone, with the result that at Baltinglass Abbey the local granite was used, taken from a quarry at Williamstown six and a half miles away. It is black felspathic mica, rather coarse grained, difficult to work because of a tendency to split in crooked lines. Lack of limestone in

County Wicklow was responsible for local slate rock mixed with rolled field stones of quartz and granite being employed in the monasteries at Glendalough. In these buildings the granite blocks are in many places corroded by the weather, whilst the slate stones in their present state indicate a great durability.

Appendix B, p. 111, describes in more detail the types of stones used by the Augustinians and Cistercians in the constructions of their abbeys and their methods of building.

D – Human factors influencing the choice of site in river valleys

It is difficult to know exactly what was in the minds of the locators or how the monks perceived their environment when they made a decision to site in one place rather than another. Nevertheless the vocational rules of the Augustinians may have been responsible for their river valley sitings:

(1) their role of giving hospitality to travellers who used the valley routes;

(2) their work of attending the sick whereby they had hospices in accessible areas perhaps on pilgrimage routes;

(3) pastoral work involving as it did the cure of souls, which led them to settle in populous areas;

(4) their active-contemplative orientation with the rule of manual work, which required that they should have some agricultural land, most likely available in river valleys.

Unfortunately there is no documentation to show what guided the Augustinians about choice of sites. Yet, if they were guided by the example of the mother house of Arrouaise in France, as the Cistercians were by Cîteaux, then the above factors were operative. But their decision on coming to Ireland to occupy a number of Celtic sites that were sometimes in close proximity to each other meant that they ignored the custom of their French abbeys of siting at selected distances.

There are, however, documents which indicate the human considerations influencing the Cistercians in their choice of sites:

(1) Whenever possible the abbey should be so laid out that everything essential was found within the enclosure walls.

(2) The site had to be inspected by four senior abbots of the Order who were required to report to the General Chapter on its suitability. Only after a favourable report would the site be approved by the Chapter.

(3) Cistercian abbeys should be located at least ten Burgundian leagues from each other.

The insistence on a site with running water, its inspection by abbots and ratification by the General Chapter influenced the Cistercians to choose river valley sites. In only one case do we find a grantor, Theobald Walter, specifying a site for an abbey namely 'the island of Arklow' thereon to erect an house for the monks of the Cistercian Order.[38] The donor may have been aware of the strict rules regarding the siting of an abbey, for the specification is immediately qualified, 'with the liberty to build the same in any other more eligible situation'.

There was an element of prestige in making a grant of land and providing a site for an abbey, particularly with regard to the Augustinians. Map 26 shows the distribution of motes in medieval Ireland. On these motes there were castles, many of whose owners donated sites to the Augustinians.[39] As a result the new foundation was often close to the founder's castle. This would have been in accord with the Augustinian tendency to settle where there was occasion for *cura animarum*. This was not so with Cistercian sites. As we mentioned above, they were to be sited far 'from the haunts of men'. A contemporary comment on the Graiguenamanagh site by Bishop Hugh de Rous of Ossory in 1202, two years before the arrival of the Cister-

58

cians from Stanley Abbey in Wiltshire described this site 'as a place of horror and of vast solitude: a cave of robbers and the lair of those who lie in wait for blood'.

MAP 26
THE DISTRIBUTION OF MOTES IN MEDIEVAL IRELAND, AFTER ORPEN

Hervey de Montmourency, who lived on Great Island, offered the Dunbrody site to Buildwas Abbey in Shropshire.[40] The abbot of Buildwas sent over a delegate to see what he was being offered. This monk rejected it, saying there was only a single oak tree near it, and advised that it be given to Dublin.

GROUP 2: ABBEYS SITED ON ISLANDS IN LAKES, BOGS, OR ON ISLANDS IN THE SEA

From a total of eighteen Augustinian and one Cistercian site, only three were new. Ten of these were transfers from Celtic allegiance, six were on abandoned Celtic sites. An island site in a lake or in a bog or in the sea was diametrically opposed to the valley bottom positions that have just been discussed. The physical size of these islands put an inflexible restraint on abbeys sited on them with regard to economic exploitation and offered few opportunities for growth.

ISLANDS IN LAKES

These islands were very small, having an average of ninety acres each (SEE FIG. 2A). The two biggest islands, Saints' Island and Inchmore, were refoundations. Furthermore, Lough Ree in the Shannon River System had four island monastic sites, inclined towards the Roscommon side of the lake. These islands were similar in that they were covered with limestone drift.

Rank	Lake	Island	Area Ac.R.P.	Trans-ferred	Re-founded	River System
1	L. Ree	Saints' Islands	203–2–9		R	Shannon
2	L. Ree	Inchcleraun	143–1–34	T		Shannon
3	L. Ree	Inchmore	132–0–32		R	Shannon
4	L. Erne	Devenish	123–0–8	T		R. Erne
5	L. Ree	Hare Is.	113–1–26	T		Shannon
6	L. Leane	Innisfallen	21–2–24	T		Leane
7	L. Gowna	Inchmore	14–2–7	T		
8	L. Derg	Saints' Islands	10–0–13	T		L. Derg
9	L. Key	Inchmacnerin	5–0–13		R	L. Key (Boyle)

FIGURE 2A

Typical of such island sites is Inchcleraun (SEE MAP 27) on Lough Ree,[41] Co. Longford. The abbey is sited on the south east shore. There are no exposures on the island but there are abundant boulders on its western shore which is strewn with (chiefly angular) blocks of dark grey limestone with bands of chert, the island being largely composed of drift. Landing is feasible on the west coast at Limekiln Harbour and on the east at Landing Stage. The site is typical of an old Celtic monastic ruin (SEE ILLUSTRATIONS 19 AND 20) with its enclosing wall round a group of old churches.

60

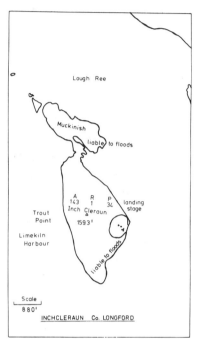

MAP 27

INCHLERAUN CO. LONGFORD

Saints' Island, Co. Donegal, is little more than ten acres
in area and is underlain by flaggy quartzites, or finely
laminated siliceous schists. The highest point on the island
is 492 feet and the abbey is towards the west shore. Access
to the island as recorded on the six inch Ordnance Survey
map, was by the 'piers of the ancient wooden bridge'
which connects with the ancient road across Portneillin-
wore Hill on the mainland (SEE MAP 28).

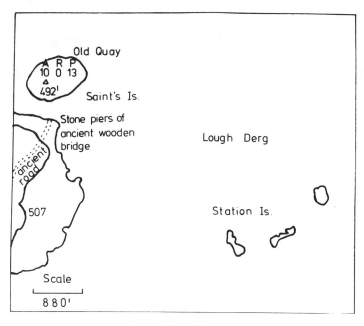

Old Quay

A R P
10 0 13
△
492'
Saint's Is.

Stone piers of
ancient wooden
bridge

ancient road

507

Lough   Derg

Station Is.

Scale

8 8 0'

MAP 28

The smallest of the islands was Church Island in Lough
Key, Co. Roscommon, on which Inchmacnerin Abbey
was sited. This island consists of shingle, chiefly red grits
and conglomerates. However, it is only about three hundred yards from the mainland and has some shelter from
the west, for its maximum altitude is one hundred fifty one
feet while the mainland rises to three hundred feet (MAP
29).

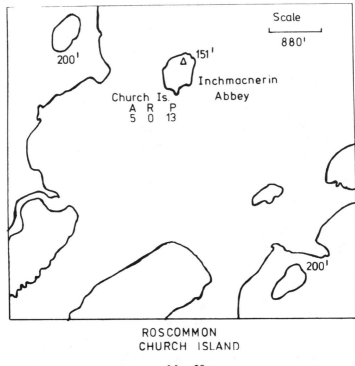

ROSCOMMON
CHURCH ISLAND

Map 29

Since the islands, by their physical size, put a restriction on the economic development and expansion of monasteries sited on them, it is difficult to appreciate fully what criteria guided Celtic monks in their choice of sites. As monks they were largely inspired by the monastic movement of the Egyptian desert. They applied the word desert (*diseart*) to many of their sites and it is obvious that islands would have given them much of the solitude and protection afforded by the desert.

63

ISLANDS IN BOGS

Of the sites in bogs, Monaincha, Co. Tipperary, Killagha, Co. Kerry, Derry (the Bogside), and Clonfert belonged to the Augustinians and Abbeydorney to the Cistercians. These were all Celtic legacy sites.

Monaincha (ILL. 21) is an island of limestone gravel about three acres in size and situated almost in the centre of a widely extended bog called the Bog of Monela. Of the three factors which determined the precise siting of an abbey—running water, solid rock, and building stone—only the firm foundation is present at this site. Building stones were brought from two districts, a grit stone from the neighbouring hills of Ballaghmore and a close textured hard grit stone, species of lapidum schistarum which splits into flags six feet long, were quarried at the south west end of the bog. This island was surrounded by water which in turn was surrounded by a vast miry shaking bog, and until one hundred and fifty years ago was accessible only by boat. All the drains and streams tributary to the River Nore that flow through the bog, were choked up until the reclamation scheme of 1920. Therefore, there must have been great labour involved in transporting the building material to the gravel island site in cots (boats) of excavated trees. Since it was an island site in bogland there was little possibility of using what is called the corduroy road, though the *togher*, alternate layers of planks and brushwood, was a recognized form of routeway through Irish bogs. This was a Celtic transfer site and some of the monks became Augustinians about 1140, whilst others remained Culdees. The Augustinians, according to Ware,[42] moved one mile south west to Corbally in 1485 because they found 'the vapours from the marshes surrounding the island unhealthy in spite of the traditional salubrity and supernatural power of the island'.

The monastery of St. Colmcille, Derry, was founded in 545 in Calgach's oak wood (where the Protestant Cathe-

64

dral stands today). This abbey continued in existence, and in 1162 Abbot Flahertach demolished over eighty houses which were 'too near the churches of Derry'[43] in order to build a great church, the Teampall Mor, (on the site of the present St. Columba's Catholic Church). This Teampall Mor had a round tower designated the Long Tower (See Map 30) and now preserved as a name on one of Derry city's streets. This abbey was sited on the north of an island of Dalradian schist, on top of which was a thin strip of boulder clay. Solid rock was close to the surface but there was no chance of running water so the monks resorted to windmills. The schists are impervious, hence the marshes noted in 'Thomas Phillip's Survey of Derry', (See Map 32)

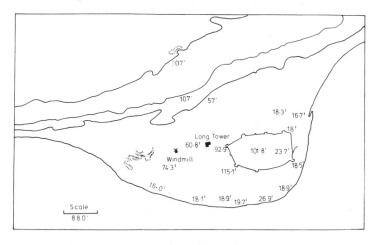

MAP 30

THE ABBEY OF DERRY

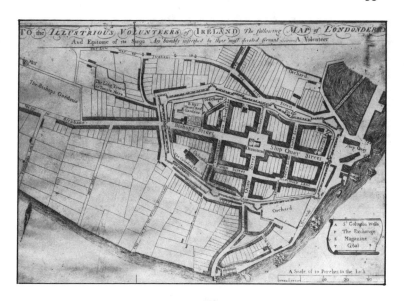

MAP 31

LONDONDERRY

(BY PERMISSION OF THE BOARD OF TRINITY COLLEGE, DUBLIN)

which especially details the island in the bogside of Derry. The map of the City of Londonderry c. 1747 indicates that 'from A to B is a drain, through the meadow, level with the surface of high tides and from that drain to the River is the island of Derry' (MAP 32). The windmill is featured in Map 31 and Map 32. On the fourth map the Long Tower, the abbey site of the Augustinians, is depicted. In Map 30 and Map 31, the windmill and the Temple Mor are shown.

MAP 32

LONDONDERRY

(BY PERMISSION OF THE BOARD OF TRINITY COLLEGE, DUBLIN)

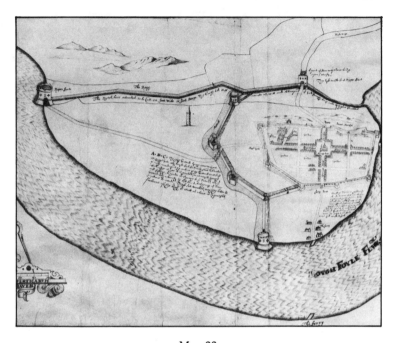

MAP 33

LONDONDERRY

(TRINITY COLLEGE DUBLIN)

Abbeydorney, Co. Kerry, was a Cistercian abbey site surrounded by marsh. In this marshland there were two elongated limestone gravel mounds standing above flood level, on the smaller of which the abbey was raised. The limestone gravel mounds provided a slight eminence above land 'liable to be flooded' according to the first edition of The Ordnance Survey Map of Ireland (c. 1830), and afforded a solid dry foundation for the abbey (SEE MAP 34). The land 'liable to be flooded' almost reaches thirty-four feet above sea-level. Today it is an area of cut away bog, the former depth of which is not known. The absence of running water made this a rather inferior type of site very unlike the traditional Cistercian choice.

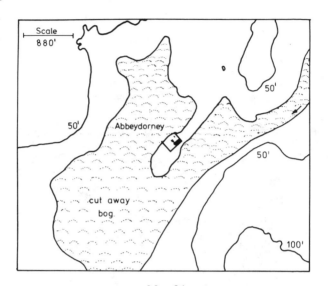

MAP 34
ABBEYDORNEY CO. KERRY

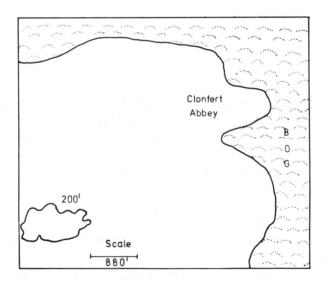

MAP 35
CLONFERT ABBEY CO. GALWAY

Some abbeys were founded on island sites which combined physical characteristics of both lake and marsh where the area in the physical sense was limited and their growth inhibited. All these physical characteristics are found combined at Errew (See Ill. 22 and 23), on a promontory projecting into Lough Corrib. The abbey is sited on a low platform of carboniferous limestone as shown by the fifty foot contour, (See Map 36) and attached to the mainland by a boggy isthmus, in the form of a low saddle. The map depicts a presque île, but this reflects a lowered water level consequent on the National Drainage Reclamation Scheme (post 1930) and the presque île today may in the Middle Ages have been a true island surrounded by water.

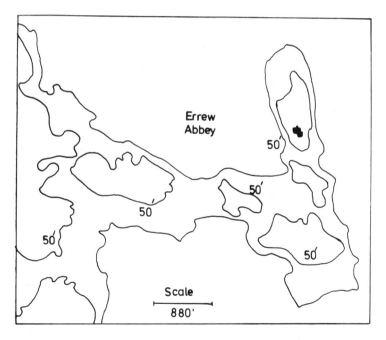

MAP 36
ERREW ABBEY CO. MAYO

A similar situation is seen at Tristernagh Abbey, Co. Westmeath, where combined physical circumstances of bog and lake give an island site. This abbey was situated on an outcrop of carboniferous limestone on a promontory projecting into Lough Iron. Lough Iron has shrunk (SEE MAP 37 ON WHICH A MAP OF 1808 HAS BEEN SUPERIMPOSED). A bench mark to the north of the abbey indicates 209 feet so that an eight foot rise in the water level would make an island-in-lake site, or a promontory island. A similar situation is indicated at Clonfert.

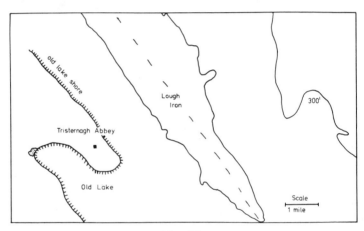

MAP 37
TRISTERNAGH ABBEY CO WESTMEATH.
THE DIMINISHING SIZE OF LOUGH IRON.

ABBEY SITES ON ISLANDS IN THE SEA

Only three abbeys belong to this category and all were Augustinian: Canon Island, St. Patrick's Island, and Molana. Of these Canon Island (SEE FIG. 2A P. 59) in the Shannon estuary was the largest being 270 acres 3 roods 27 perches in extent. The abbey was sited on an outcrop of carboniferous limestone to the north east of the island. St.

Patrick's Island, in the Irish Sea eight miles out from
Dublin, was a Patrician site. It is a small island of only
seventeen acres with a rocky foreshore all around and a
cliff coast on the east. The church lay to the south, with
the higher ground rising to the west to a spot height of sixty
feet. In 1220 Archbishop Henry of London moved the
community of St. Patrick's Island to the mainland to
Holmpatrick.[44]

Molana Abbey was founded on an island to the north of
the confluence of the Glendine and Blackwater Rivers.
This place remained an island until 1850, when the owner
of Ballynatry Desmesne (G. Smyth)[45] drained the channel
and joined it to the mainland.

GROUP 3: ABBEY SITES ON DRUMLINS

There were ten abbeys sited on drumlins, seven of which
were Celtic legacy sites; this implies that neither order
favoured drumlins as sites for new abbeys. Drumlins are
ice moulded ridges, and the drumlin belt is an inescapable
physiographic aspect of the Irish landscape, with no mor-
phological boundry. The drumlin belt in Ireland stretches
from Belfast Lough and the neighbourhood of Dundalk
across the whole of Ireland to Donegal, Sligo, and Clew
Bay, an area of roughly one hundred miles by forty miles,
approximately 4,000 square miles. There are also isolated
swarms in the Lower Bann Valley, in various lowlands in
north and west Donegal, and far to the south around Ban-
try Bay. The nature of drumlins varies; some are rounded
hills of boulder clay, some have rock cores with a covering
of drift and between these two types there is every grada-
tion of drumlin so that it is not possible in many cases to
make a clear distinction between actual drumlins and
ground moraine. The height of the drumlins also varies: in
some places they stand up as single individual hills; in
other areas they are in an impacted series; or indeed two

drumlins may coalesce. Drainage is impeded everywhere, hence between the drumlins there are numerous lakes and ponds that are being steadily filled by silt. Some such ponds have been replaced by a fen or bog peat. Again with regard to the alignment of drumlins, there is no general direction, the pattern of distribution is varied. Thus on the whole the drumlins present a landscape of numerous little hills with highly varied conditions of soil and drainage.

At Armagh the abbey of St. Peter and Paul (See Map 38) was one of several churches on a drumlin, the bedrock of which was carboniferous limestone with a ten foot covering of boulder clay. On this drumlin was a civitas which has been previously referred to in this paper but not described cartographically. It is to be found on Bartlett's [46] map which is a reproduction of a sixteenth century map of Armagh, one of a collection of twenty-three maps found in London in 1956 by Dr. J.Bowlby, who presented them to the National Library of Ireland. (Map 38).

Bartlett's map shows an aerial view across the historic mound or rath of Armagh looking west. Hayes McCoy, who has edited this collection of maps, identifies the church buildings of this civitas as follows: the ruined church within the curiously shaped rath or enclosure in the left foreground must be Templefartagh, AD 445, which is claimed as a site of the original Patrician church at Armagh and the possible burial place of St. Patrick. The Patrician church is said to have been built within an enclosure at the foot of the eminence on which stood Daire's rath of Armagh, called the Sally Ridge. The path leading by this ruin towards the conspicuous standing cross is roughly in line of the present Scotch Street and Market Street. This cross is now preserved within the cathedral. Behind the cross is the gateway of the inner rath. The walls of this rath extend right and left around the hill following the contour. The large building centrally placed within the rath is the Cathedral. Also within the inner rath are two houses of Irish type, the ruin of a long building of rectangular ground

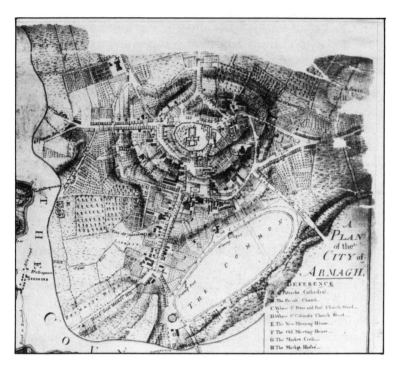

MAP 38
(TRINITY COLLEGE DUBLIN)

plan lying to the south of the cathedral which may have
been the Culdee Priory (AD 921) and the table-like structure which may be a tomb. Outside the inner rath, in the
extreme south of the picture, there is a Franciscan Friary
(AD 1263); between this and the Culdee Priory is the ruin
of a small church which was Templebreda, the house of
the Nuns. Behind the Cathedral, surrounded by more
Irish houses, was the house and church of the Augustinians of Armagh (AD 1126). To the north of the Cathedral is
the ruin of St. Columba's Church. In the distance, and to
the west beside the road leading by Emhain Macha, stands
a small ruin that may be Templemurry. This drumlin site
was given to St. Patrick by Daire, Lord of the territory.

Why the saint took it is not known. The human factor that one and a half miles to the west was Navan fort, the seat of the ancient kings of the prehistoric Fifth of Ulster may have influenced his choice. Map 38 shows the ecclesiastical and secular features of a civitas that evolved between the fifth and fifteenth century and it is intriguing to the historical geographer to see the migratory movement of the monastic sites up the slopes of the drumlin. The Patrician church of the fifth century was sited on the lower slope just above the inter-drumlin margin, the Culdee Priory of 921 inside the rath on the middle of the slope, and finally the Cathedral perched on the top of the drumlin at two hundred thirty-one feet and the church of St. Peter and St. Paul founded for the Augustinians in 1126, at two hundred feet.

This drumlin offered a dry site to the ecclesiastical builders. The enclosures on the slopes of the drumlin and the heaps of stone between them are earthworks made by excavating ditches and throwing up the soil to form banks, a not too difficult job in the ten foot covering of boulder clay. Bartlett called these enclosures Trians, the Trian Saxon was on the extreme right, the Trian Masain in the centre and the Trian Mor around Teampall na Fearta. For the Augustinians there was a human attraction in the pastoral work, the *cura animarum* afforded in the Trians for this drumlin featured an ecclesiastical centre site near a secular site. A difficulty of this site however was low water potential. Wells could be sunk into the water-bearing sandstones of the Cathedral site and also to the south of it, but there was no running water for power. From the Augustinian Abbey to the nearest river, the Callan, is one and a half miles and the descent of the drumlin slope from two hundred thirty-one feet at the top to one hundred nine feet at the banks of the Callan was too steep a gradient to allow water to be drawn up from the river to the abbey site. Therefore instead of water mills, wind mills were used (See Map 38).

MAP 39

ARMAGH

REPRODUCED FROM *Ulster and other Irish Maps, c. 1600*
BY PERMISSION OF THE IRISH MANUSCRIPTS COMMISSION, DUBLIN.

Movilla Abbey, Co. Down, (See Map 40) was a Celtic site that was refounded, the founders being motivated by sentiment rather than by the quality of the site. It was sited on a single drumlin (Ill. 23).

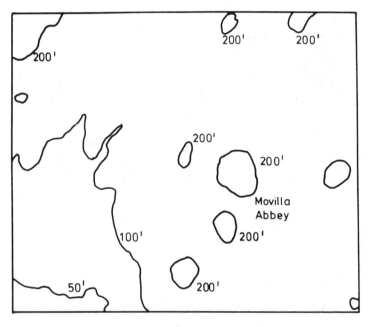

MAP 40

MOVILLA ABBEY CO. DOWN

The core of which is greywacke, a combination of mudstone and gritstone, with a covering of boulder clay. These rocks are impervious so a water supply must have been difficult to obtain. There is no river on which to site a mill, hence the windmill, and building stone had to be brought from Scrabo quarries two miles distant.

The Cathedral at Clogher, Co. Tyrone, occupies the site of the former Augustinian abbey. It is situated to the north east of a drumlin of boulder clay on carboniferous limestone (See Ill. 25) overlooking the River Blackwater,

which, in the vicinity of the site, is flowing from south
west to north east. These rocks belong to the Clogher Valley shale group, and would under normal conditions carry
water, but a forty foot overlay of drift made it difficult to
exploit this. As is typical in a drumlin landscape, the river
is meandering (See Map 41) but the meander loops could be
by-passed by a mill race. Building stone in the form of
hard massive yellow sandstone was obtained one mile
southwards and coarse red sandstones, three miles northwards.

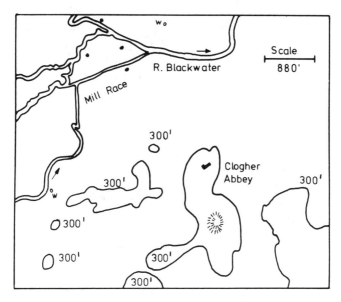

MAP 41

CLOGHER ABBEY CO. TYRONE

78

Saul Abbey (SEE MAP 42), Co. Down, is in an area of impacted drumlins, which display typical inter-drumlin marsh.

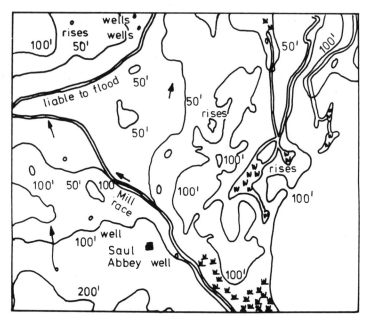

MAP 42
SAUL ABBEY CO. DOWN

The Quoile River flows along their base. The Abbey is sited on a drumlin of solid greywacke with ten feet of boulder clay on top. The marshland in the vicinity of this drumlin may be the relict remains of an earlier lake. The impervious nature of the rock has been responsible for the number of wells in this district, the most famous of which are 'Struell Wells'. The drumlin slopes provide a surface runoff in the form of streamlets which collect in the inter-drumlin hollows in ponds or lakes. From such a lake south of Saul emerges a stream, the Slaneyburn, the volume of which was adequate to drive the mills of Saul once a mill-race was dug. The solid rock on which this abbey was built was only ten feet below the surface. Nevertheless this area of impacted drumlins, of interdrumlin marsh with damp valley bottom soils, did not provide an attractive physical environment for an abbey; it was not a normal river valley siting. It was a Patrician site taken over by anchorites in Celtic times, and was refounded by St. Malachy when he was Bishop of Down. Saul derives from *Sabhal*, a 'barn' which was given to St. Patrick for his first church by Dichiu, his first convert in Ulster.

In conslusion, abbeys sited in drumlins were of variable quality depending on (1) the nature of the bedrock and whether it was pervious or impervious, (2) the depth of the drift, (3) the nature of the inter-drumlin area: whether occupied by a fen, marsh, pond, or river. The rivers in such areas have a tendency to meander, which makes them unsuitable for water power, although in some cases they could be engineered and used. The height of individual drumlins did, however, facilitate the use of windmills. Building stone in many cases was not available. There were no rock exposures, so stone had to be brought from a distance, as at the Movilla Abbey site for which stone was brought from Scrabo, two miles distant, and this must have involved overland haulage as there is no convenient river.

GROUP 4: MISCELLANEOUS

This category includes a group of abbeys consisting of (1) coastal abbeys, including those on sea cliffs, and (2) those on esker sites, ridge sites, mountain slopes. In this category there were twenty abbeys of which the Augustinians had seven coastal and the Cistercians five. The remainder were ungrouped and individualistic. The coastal sites were the biggest single group in this category and these will be dealt with first.

COASTAL

The term coastal implies a site from which the sea is visible. The sites within this group are less than one mile from tidal water. Tables 11–16 (pp. 129–133) show that of the coastal sites six were new and six were Celtic legacy.

Aughris was a cliff site on a stormy headland in close proximity to the sea and to tidal waters. The early Celtic monastery had close connections with the Celtic monastery of Inishmurry, whose monks are thought to have migrated to Aughris after the Norse raids of the ninth century, and the refounded monastery of St. Mary's Aughris continued to use the name Insula Mury or equivalents till the fifteenth century.

Bangor Abbey, Co. Down, on the contrary, did not occupy a stormy headland but was sited on a slight eminence of less than one hundred feet overlooking Bangor Bay. This abbey was five hundred yards from the highwater mark of the tide. It rests on boulder clay, and is not a very good site. A better place would have been eight hundred yards to the west of this where there is a sand and gravel belt and where the Bryans Burn stream would have provided suitable water power. It is possible that the monks built where they did because the greywacke stone they used is available within one hundred yards of the site.

Ballysadare Abbey, Co. Sligo, (MAP 43) was one hundred seventeen feet from the high water mark of the tide.

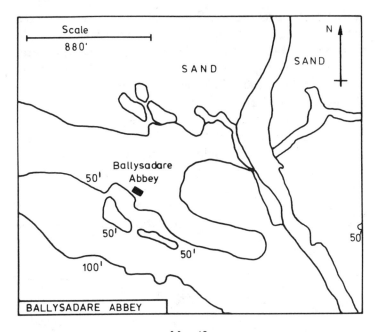

MAP 43
BALLYSADARE ABBEY CO. SLIGO

  The coast at high tide undergoes very severe erosion. The
early Celtic monastery founded by St. Feichin was built
on the left bank of the Ballysadare River, which is flowing
northwards while the abbey for the Augustinians was
built two hundred thirty yards to the west of this; although
the Celtic site would have been better, it may not have
been offered to the Augustinians. The abbey was sited on
solid rock and the Ballysadare River, excellent for water
power, was only four hundred yards to the east of it.

  Corcomroe Cistercian Abbey, Co. Clare, cannot be
seen from the sea nor can the sea be seen from the abbey,
(MAP 44 AND ILL. 26).

It is sited at less than a hundred feet above sea level, and
Abbey Hill with its prolongation westwards screens the
abbey from the sea. This site was obviously chosen because

of the shelter provided by the hill against the westerly sea winds. The abbey is built on an outcrop of rock ('Karst') in a dry valley named Priests' Valley. There is a well there, Tobershela, but no river. A winter resurgence—a spring of water in an area of porous rocks in a wet winter— makes it a peculiar siting for Cistercians, but they may have simply taken the Celtic site as they found it.

From Cape Clear to Waterford Harbour on the south coast of Ireland, there are long stretches of cliff as much as two hundred feet high, broken only by drowned valleys and inlets of small streams deeply set in the lowland or coastal peneplane. Near Courtmacsherry, Co. Cork, there is a pre-glacial raised beach. Hereabouts, the pre-Ice Age

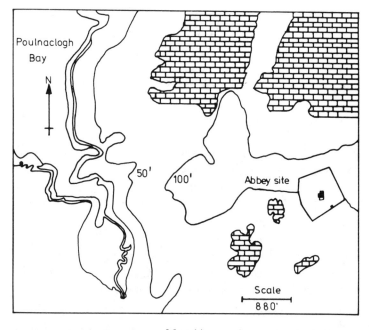

MAP 44

CORCUMROE ABBEY CO. CLARE

coastline followed the line of the present one, but the sea level was a bit higher, so the old beach appears as a platform above the present high tide mark along the coast of West Cork. On this shelf there are some glacial deposits which indicate that the plateau itself is pre-glacial. In the bay of Courtmacsherry on the left bank and on such a broad platform, Maure Abbey (Abbey Mahon) was sited (Map 45).

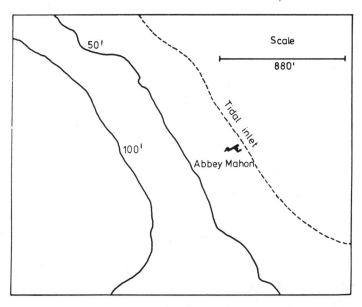

MAP 45
ABBEY MAHON CO. CORK

It stands at sixteen feet above the high water mark of the tide, on a platform one hundred seventy-six feet wide. A convex slope rises two hundred feet from the platform toward the north. Its width was somewhat restricted and confined although it provided a dry site on solid rock. This abbey is referred to in the Statute of 1281 as having failed and been restored. Abbeystrowry (Map 46) was presumably founded after 1228 and after experiencing initial failure was restored as an abbey after 1281.

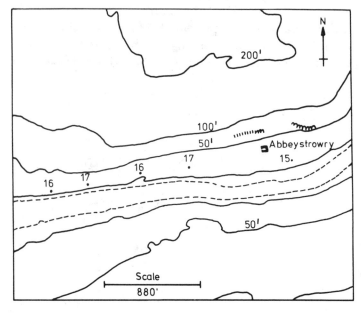

MAP 46

ABBEYSTROWRY

This was not a success either, for it was reduced to being a cell of Abbeymahon previously described.

Inch Abbey (MAP 47 AND ILL. 27) and Grey Abbey (MAP 48 AND ILL. 28) were two Cistercian foundations in Co. Down on the shore of Strangford Lough. Inch was a Celtic abbey whose members became Cistercian. The word 'Inch' means a place near a river which is subject to flooding so the name itself implies this circumstance. This abbey was sited on the south east of a gentle drumlin above a thin strip of river alluvium overlooking the Quoile River not far from the Quoile inundation line.

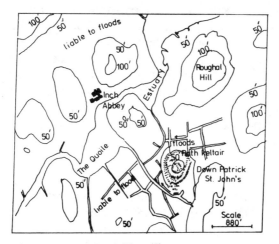

MAP 47

INCH ABBEY CO. DOWN

Grey Abbey was founded by Africa, wife of John de Courcy and daughter of Godfred, King of Man.

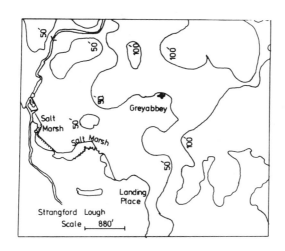

MAP 48

GREY ABBEY CO. DOWN

It also is on the slope of a gentle drumlin of approximately fifty feet, overlooking the salt marshes of Strangford Lough. The abbey is sited on thin boulder clay over a bedrock of greywacke, the solid rock being very near to the surface. This is a peculiar site for a Cistercian abbey, for it rests on a drumlin with no river near it and there would be no chance of obtaining water through the boulder clay. The building stone was the local silurian grit and new red sandstone dressings were obtained from three quarters of a mile away.

HILL SLOPES

Kilcooley Abbey, Co. Tipperary, founded for the Cistercians by Donal Mor O'Brien, King of Munster, was on a very unusual site (MAP 49 AND ILL. 29). It was on a hill slope of the Slieve Ardagh Mountains at over four hundred feet, far from a suitable river.

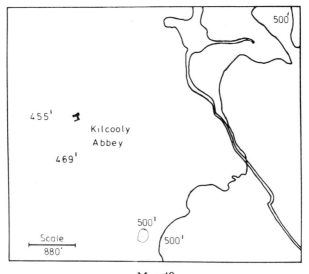

MAP 49
KILCOOLEY ABBEY, CO. TIPPERARY

The aerial photograph (ILL. 32) 'taken in late evening sunshine, when low earthworks and disturbed ground not easily visible in ordinary light are detectable, has revealed the exact position of the early monastery. A circular rath like enclosure two hundred feet across with two ditches is clearly discernible some short distance in front of the Cistercian ruins. It is unquestionably the site of the first monastery—perhaps of the early sixth century Daire Mor mentioned in the Annals. Evident traces of disturbed land all around suggests that the original earthen enclosure walls were levelled by the first Cistercians for agricultural purposes in the twelfth century'.[47]

Roscommon Augustinian Abbey was sited on a drift ridge of two hundred feet that is underlain by almost horizontal beds of limestone. In the townland of Ballypheasan and Lochvaneane, some thirty feet lower than the ridge, are what are called the "bottom lands". On Map 50 the Ordnance Survey Map has been superimposed on the geological map and it shows that these bottom lands are turloughs, lakes that appear when the water table rises and disappears when it falls.

The lakes may have been more permanent before the modern improved drainage schemes were introduced, and the drift ridge on which the abbey was sited would have provided a dry routeway to the north east and south west of Ireland.

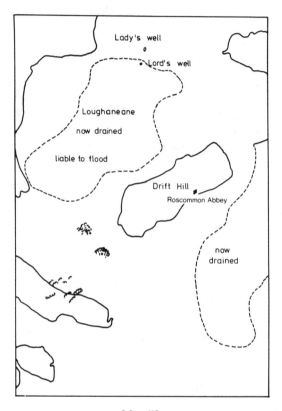

MAP 50

Illustration 31 is an aerial photograph of Kilmacduagh, Co. Galway, on a low elongated limestone hill. It is a dry site, but to the east there is marsh. Reference to the geology map shows that this is due to turloughs and despite the time of the year indicated by cereal cultivation, the turloughs are still visible. This site is peculiar and is therefore included in the miscellaneous category.

Kilshanny Abbey, Co. Clare, Muckamore, Co. Antrim, and Jerpoint, Co. Kilkenny, were three elevated sites. Kilshanny is situated at one hundred eleven feet on the crest of an elongated hill, in fact, almost on an interfluve between the Carrowkeel River and a tributary (MAP 51).

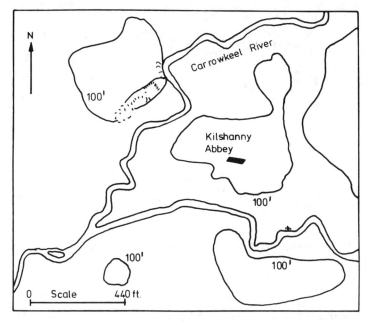

MAP 51
KILSHANNEY ABBEY CO. CLARE

This formation is almost uniclinal with a steep side on the north presenting an almost scarp-like slope in that direction. The underlying rock is sandstone and the chasm-like passage to the east between the one hundred feet contours is the result of erosion, the Carrowkeel River probably flowed south at one time instead of turning west as it does now at St. Augustines' Well. This is a kame, and its peculiar elevation makes one wonder why the monks chose it as a site, especially when a river site was available in close proximity. There is no evidence to show that it had previously been a Celtic site.

Muckamore Abbey site (MAP 52), Co. Antrim, was excavated in August 1973.

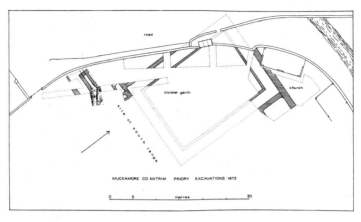

MAP 52

MUCKAMORE CO. ANTRIM PRIORY EXCAVATIONS 1973

This abbey was on the left bank of the Six Mile Water and the site is mapped as a river terrace. This terrace is a gravel and sand moraine which runs from Antrim to south of Doagh. This site is flat, one hundred feet high, and is dry. The river has many riffles, with basaltic rock barriers in its bed, but it is suitable for water power. The drift, which is forty feet thick, is underlain by basalt. One of the difficulties of this left bank site at such an elevation was the problem of a domestic water supply. Excavations reveal that water from slope run-off was led by a stone-lined conduit to a cobbled reservoir. There is no evidence to show that conduits were contrived to lead the water through the south range of buildings. The domestic water must therefore have been lifted manually. Adjacent to the reservoir is a necessarium, and water from the reservoir was used to flush sewage from it into the river. A left bank elevated site was a disadvantage where domestic water supply was concerned.

Jerpoint Abbey, Co. Kilkenny, was on an elevated site within a valley overlooking a river rather than at the

valley bottom. This abbey is on the right bank of the Arrigle River, four hundred forty yards south of its confluence with the River Nore. Here there is a thin strip of limestone gravel over coarse Old Red Sandstone. The Nore is
meandering at this part of its course, the gradient is small,
and the river has a low head. The Arrigle reaches base level before joining the Nore, its momentum so decreasing
that the abbey was sited well above the fall line on a veri-
table cliff. Recent excavations show that a domestic water
supply was led from the Arrigle river's millstream (see Map
53).

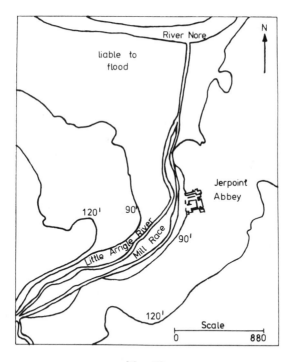

MAP 53
JERPOINT ABBEY CO. KILKENNY

Such a siting is peculiar in being on an elevation rather than in a valley (SEE ILL. 32). However, this was a Celtic site with a transfer of Celtic personnel to the Cistercian Order and so was a legacy site.[48] Nevertheless if the Cistercians had found this to be an unsuitable site they could have moved it down to the banks of the Nore, as this land was included on the abbey charter in the original endowment of lands. However, the presence of a side stream, a dry site, and an existing Celtic nucleus was an attractive enough proposition and accounts for its cliff rather than valley bottom position but Jerpoint is unusual and amounts to the exception proving the rule.

CONCLUSION

The purpose of this study has been to trace the foundation of the monasteries established in medieval Ireland by the Cistercians and the Canons Regular of St Augustine, both orders introduced by St Malachy. This has involved an interweaving of physical and historical geography. The spiritual orientations of the Order have not been investigated, though the monks' social relations with the people were touched on, as, in the case of the Augustinian Canons, were their ministerial duties. The Canons did pastoral work as part of their vocation and though they, like the Cistercians, possessed lands, they drew part of their income from the dues or tithes given by the people in return for their pastoral ministry. The contemplative Cistercians, to whom pastoral ministry was forbidden by their constitutions, settled in places remote from population centres. Elsewhere I have studied the buildings erected on these sites, the lands possessed by these orders and their exploitation of them, and, in the case of the Canons Regular, the ownership of churches.

The Celtic system which preceded their introduction was studied to investigate how far these new orders grafted onto its network. In many cases both orders settled either on sites that had been abandoned or were low in personnel and willing to change over to the new observances. Thirteen of the Cistercians and fifty-seven of the Canons Regular were located on such sites.

The general distribution of the monasteries was examined with regard to altitude of sites, their locations on major routeways, and the distribution of population. A physical classification of sites based on the main topographical features of Ireland: river valleys; islands in rivers, island in the sea, island in bogs; drumlins and a miscellaneous group which included eskers, kames, and coastal sites. This revealed that the Cistercians had twenty-five valleys bottom sites out of thirty-four houses, whilst the Canons Regular had fifty out of ninety-six similarly chosen, their remaining forty being on islands in rivers, islands in bogs, on drumlins, eskers, or the coast. Such sites would have been too restrictive for the Cistercians with their requirements for self-support and self-sufficiency. On the other hand, the fact that the Augustinian Canons accepted tithes, staffed churches, had hospices, did pastoral work, and were not wholly dependent on manual work or the exploitation of land meant that the comprehensive nature of their work allowed for this diversity. Although we do not know what was in the minds of the locators, nor do we know how they perceived their environment, we can, with the aid of text, maps, photographs, tables, and diagrams, begin to glimpse the enormously influential roles of the celtic system and the physical geographical factors governing the selection of sites by the Canons Regular and the Cistercians in Medieval Ireland.

APPENDIX A

FIELD WORK: INSPECTION OF MONASTIC SITES
KEY

(1) No river present 2 (1)NRP; River present = (1)RP.
(2) Bank on which abbey is situated (2)R = Right bank;
      (2)L = Left bank.
(3) The shortest distance from abbey ruin to bank of river
      = (3) . . . feet.
(4) Width of stream at abbey ridge (if there is one) = (4) . . . feet.
(5) Rock exposures along river banks = (5)EX; no exposures
      = (5)NEX.
(6) Point bars and riffles in the river = (6)PB/R; no point bars and
      riffles = (6)NPB/R.
(7) Minor Stream = (7)MS; Major River = (7)MR; Minor stream
      tributary to a major river = (7)MSTM.
(8) Island in lake = (8)IL; island in bog = (8)IB; promontory
      island = (8)PI; promontory island in lake = (8)PIL;
      promontory island in bog = (8)PIB; drumlins = (8)D;
      Miscellaneous = (8)M.
(9) Break of slope = (9)BS; Flood limit line denoted by riverine
      sand = (9)RS; flag irises = (9)FI.
(10) Chancel end of building due east = (10)E;
      not due east = (10)NE.
(11) Dry site = (11)DS; wet boulder clay = (11)WBC; wet site
      = (11)WS; thick drift site = (11)THD; thin drift =
      (11)TD; Marsh = (11)M.
(12) Buildings of local rock = (12)LR; imported material = (12)IM;
      considerable remains = (12)CR; few remains = (12)FR; no
      extant remains = (12)NER.
(13) Topography: with regard to the surrounding countryside where
      there were hills, drumlins, kames, eskers, was the abbey situated
      on the most elevated site or not?
      Abbey on highest eminence = (13)HE;
      Abbey not on highest eminence = (13)NHE.
(14) Any evidence of cut away bog = (14)CB; Any evidence of
      nearby bog = (14)B; No bog in evidence = (14)NB.

Abbeyderg:
   (1)RP; (2)R; (3) 300 feet; (4) 10 feet; (5)NEX; (6)NPB/R; (7)MS; (11)DS; (12)LR; (13)NHE.

Abbeygormacan:
   (1)RP; (2)L; (3) 60 feet; (4) 10 feet; (5)NEX; (6)NPB/R; (7)MS; (11)BC; (12)LR; (13)NHE; (14)NB.

Aghmacart:
   (1)RP; (2)R; (3) 1140 feet; (4) 3 feet; (5)EX; (6)NPB/R; (7)MS; (11)DS; (12)LR; (14)NB.

Annaghdown:
   (1)NRP; (5)NEX; (8)PIL; (11)THD; (12)LR; (13)NHE; (14)CB.

Armagh:
   (1)NRP; (5)NEX; (8)D; (11)DS; (12)NER; (13)NHE; (14)NB.

Athassel:
   (1)RP; (2)R; (3) 60 feet; (4) 40 feet; (5)EX; (6)NPB/R; (7)MR; (11)DS; (12)LR-IM; (14)NB.

Aughrim:
   (1)RP; (2)R; (3) 500 feet; (4) 10 feet; (5)EX; (6)NPB; (7)MS; (11)TD; (12)LR; (12)NER.

Aughris:
   (1)RP; (2)L; (3) 176 yards from coast; (5)EX; (6)NPB/R; (8)M; (9)FL; (11)MA; (12)LR; (13)HE.

Ballintubber:
   (1)RP; (2)R; (3) 70 feet; (4) 10 feet; (5)EX; (6)NPB/R; (7)MS; (11)DS; (12)CR; (13)NHE; (14)B.

Ballybeg:
   (1)RP; (2)PB; (3) 200 feet; (4) 10 feet; (5)EX; (6)NPB/R; (7)MS; (11)DS; (12)LR; (13)NHE; (14)   (12)CR; (To the south is a dry valley)..

Ballyboggan:
   (1)RP; (2)L; (3) 45 feet; (4) 60 feet; (5)NE; (6)NPB/R; (7)MS; (9) adjacent to gravel esker, site liable to be flooded by Boyne; (10)E; (11)WS; (12) Sandstone; (14)NB.

Ballysadare:
   (1)RP; (2)L; (3) 880 feet; (4) 117 feet from coast; (5)EX; (6)NPB; (8)M; (11)DS; (12)LR; (12)CR; (13)HE; (14)NB.

Bangor:
   (1)NRP; (5)EX; (8)M; (11)DS; (12)FR; (13)NHE; (14)NB.

Bridgetown:
(1)RP; (2)L; (3) 15 feet; (5)EX; (6)PB/R; (7)MSTM; (10)E;
(11)DS; (12)LR; (12)CR; (13)NHE; (14)NB.

Caher:
(1)RP; (2)R; (3) 176 feet; (5)EX; (6)NPB/R; (7)MSTM; (9)BS;
(10)E; (11)DS; (12)LR; (12)CR; (14)NB.

Clogher:
(1)RP; (5)NEX; (8)D; (11)WBC; (12)FR; (13)NHE; (14)NB.

Clones:
(1)NRP; (5)NEX; (8)D; (11)WBC; (11)M; (12)FR; (13)HE.

Clonfert:
(1)NRP; (8)IB; (12)FR; (12)LR; (13)NHE; (14)B.

Clonmacnoise:
(1)RP; (2)R; (3) 500 feet; (6)NPB/R; (8)M; (12)CR; (13)NHE;
(14)B.

Clontuskert-Omanny:
(1)RP; (2)R; (2) 300 feet; (4) 15 feet; (5)NEX; (6)NPB/R; (7)MR;
(10)E; (11)FL; (12)LR; (12)CR; (13)NHE; (14)NB.

Cloontuskertnasina:
(1)RP; (2)R; (3) 528 feet; (5)NE; (6)NPB/R; (7)MR; (11)DSG;
(12)FR; (13)NHE; (14)CB.

Cong:
(1)RP; (5)EX; (6)NPB/R; (7)MSTM; (10)E; (11)DS; (12)CR;
(13)NHE; (14)NB.

Corbally:
(1)NRP; (8)M; (11)DSG; (12)FR; (13)NHE; (14)NB.

Derry:
(1)NRP; (8)IB; (11) WBC 10 feet thick on Dalradian schist.
(12)NER; (13)NHE.

Down:
(1)RP; (2)R; (3) 100 feet; (4) 15 feet; (5)EXP; (6)NPB/R;
(7)MSTM; (11)DS; (12)LR; (12)FR; (13)NHE; (14)NB.

Downpatrick (St. John's):
(1)RP; (3) ½ mile; (8)D; (11)WBC; (11)M; (12)NER; (13)NHE;
(14)NB.

Duleek:
(1)RP; (2)R; (3) 1233 feet; (5)NEX; (6)NPB/R; (7)MS; (10)E;
(11)DSG; (12)LR; (14)NB.

Dungiven:
>   (1)RP; (2)R; (3) 100 feet; (4) 60 feet; (5)NEX; (6)NPB/R; (7)MR;
>   (9)BS; (10)E; (11)DS; sandry drift over carboniferous sandstone;
>   (14)NB.

Durrow:
>   (1)RP; (2)R; (3) 60 feet; (5)BEX; (6)NPB/R; (7)MS; (11)DGS;
>   (12)FR; (14)NB.

Errew:
>   (1)NR; (5)NEX; (8) presque ile, L. Conn; (10)E; (12)LR;
>   (12)CR; (14)NB.

Ferns:
>   (1)RP; (2)R; (3) 160 feet; (5)EX; (7)MSTM; (11)DS; (14)NB.

Fertagh:
>   (1)RP; (2)L; (3) 1760 feet; (4) 10 feet; (5)EX; (6)NPB/R; (7)MS;
>   (11)DS; (12)LR; (12)FR; (14)NB.

Gallen:
>   (1)RP; (2)L; (3) 525 feet; (4) 40 feet; (5)NE; (6)NPB/R; (7)MR;
>   (11) Boulder clay, thick limestone gravel over carboniferous
>   limestone; spoil heaps 20 feet high along the Brosna bank result-
>   ing from National Drainage Scheme. Little sign of poaching by
>   grazing bullocks. (12)FR – cross-erected to mark former grave-
>   yard.

Great Connell:
>   (1)RP; (2)R; (3) 1144 feet; (4) 20 feet; (5)NEX; (6)NPB/R; (7)MR;
>   (11)DS limestone gravel; (12)FR; (14)NB; (½ mile distant); 3
>   prong gravel esker; adjacent field was ploughed and revealed a
>   six inch soil cover over a corase pebble limestone deposit.

Inistoioge:
>   (1)RP; (2)L; (3) 441 feet from R. Nore 90 feet from R. Coom;
>   (5)EX; (6)NPB/R; (7)MSTM; Strike of rock NE–SE – (10)E;
>   (11)DS; (12)CR; (13)NHE; (14)NB. There is a mote 140 yards
>   to the SW which belonged to Thos. Fitz Anthony. The mote is
>   piled up on a rock, which juts out from high ground above the
>   river valley. On the river side the mote is inaccessible and on the
>   landward side where it was not so high, it was defended by a
>   deep trench.

Kells (Antrim):
>   (1)RP; (2)LB; (3) 70 feet; (4) 20 feet; (5)EX; (6) Basaltic beds in
>   river. (7)MR; (10)E; (11)DS; (12)FR; (14)NB.

98

Kells (Kilkenny):
(1)RP; (2)R; (3) 45 feet; (4) 40 feet; (5)EX; (6)PB/R; (7)MR;
(10)E; (11)DS; (12) Plan of this abbey is unique, outside the enclosure on the south side is another wall which encloses a 2½
acre site. This is called the Burgesses Court; (14)NB.

Killagh:
(1)RP; (5)EX; (8)IB; formerly surrounded by a flooded area;
(12)CR; (14)NB.

Killeigh:
(1)RP; (3) 264 feet; (5)E; (7)MSTM; (10)E; (11)DS; (12)LR;
(14)NB. An entrenchment has been made around the site, the
field pattern is circuitous to this entrenchment.

Kilmacduagh:
(1)NRP; (5)EX; (8)M; (10)E; (11)DS; (12)LR; (12)CR;
(14) Marshy nearby.

Kilmore:
(1)NR; (5)NEX; (7)MS; (11)DS; (12)NER; (14)NB. base of
round tower not recorded on 6″ O.S.map.

Kilshanny:
(1)RP; (2)L; (3) 1500 feet; (4) 15 feet; (5)NEX; (6)NPB/R; (7)M;
(10)E; (12)LR.

Kame:
Carboniferous shales overlying sandstones (111′ A.S.L.). The
abbey was on the crest of this low elongated Kame, the drift was
at least seven feet thick, the local grave digger had never
reached rock when excavating graves. The formation was almost
uniclinal with a steep side on the northern side, the quality of
the surrounding land was poor.

Knock:
(1)NR; (3) Glyde 5280 feet; (4) 9 feet; (5)NEX; (12) not a trace
remains, it was situated three fields west of Thomastown castle.
The present owner of Thomastown Castle is called O'Reilly. His
father changed the name of Thomastown Castle to Knock Abbey
Castle to perpetuate its memory, but the 1840 and 1908 edition
of the 6″ Ordnance Survey maps adhered to the original titles.

Lisgoole:
(1)RP; (2)L; (12)NER; (5)EX; (7)MR.

Louth Abbey:
(1)RP; (3) 615 feet; (4) 3 feet; (5)NE; (6)NPB/R; (7)MS; (10)E;

(11)DS; peripheral to the site there is much evidence of marsh reeds; rushes surrounding the site – rising ground to 112'; (12)LR; (12)CR; (14)NB.

Lorrha:

(1)RP; (2)LB; (3) 450 feet; (4) 10 feet; (5)NEX; (6)NPB/R; (7)MS; (10)E; (11)DS; thick boulder clay and gravel deposit; (12)FR; (13)NHE; (14)NB.

Mayo:

(1)RP; (2)R; (3) 50 feet; (4) 10 feet; (7)NS; (5)EX; (11)LR; (12)FR; (13)NHE.

Molana:

(1)RP; (2)R; (3) 60 feet; (4) 15 feet; (5)EX; (6)NPB/R; (8)D; (12)NER; (13)NHE.

Monaincha/island in bog site:

Access is via a causeway, drainage undertaken three generations ago by a family named Maher. Today only dykes and ditches are obvious. The abbey was built on a rock outcrop. (10)E; (11)LR; This site was surrounded by a rampart six feet high, the plinth of the building is still visible, the perimeter of the rampart is 150 feet. The flood limit line denoted by rushes, sedges, flag irises was twenty yards from rampart. The land was of negative quality.

Mothel:

(1)RP; (2)L; (3) 50 feet; (4) 10 feet; (5)EX; (6)NPB/R; (7)MS; (11)LR; (12)FR; (14)NB.

Movilla:

(1)NRP; (3) distance from low water mark tide 1 mile; (8)D; (10)E; (11)WBC; (12)CR; (12)LR; (13)NHE; (14)NB.

Muckamore:

(1)RP; The site is mapped as a river terrace of the Six Mile Water. It is flat high and drey. The terrace is probably a gravel and sand moraine running from Antrim to S. of Doagh. The drift which is 40 feet thick is underlain by basalt.

Mullingar:

(1)RP; (2)R; (3) 440 feet; (5)NE; (6)NPB/R; (7)MR; (12)NER; (14)CB. Geology map Westmeath 19/3 indicates bogland before the cutting of the Grand Canal.

Navan:

(1)RP; (2)R; (3) 179 feet; (4) 150 feet; (5)EX; (7)MR; (12)NER;

On the left bank is a river cliff. The site is 300 yards west of the Boyne/Blackwater confluence..

Newtown Trim:

(1)RP; (2)L; (3) 60 feet; (4) 100 feet; (5)EX; (6)NPB/R; (7)MR; (10)E; (11)DS; (12)CR; (13)Slight Eminence; (14)NB.

Rathkeale:

(1)RP; (2)R; (3) 2640 feet; (4) 20 feet; (5)NEX; (6)NPB/R; (7)MSTM; (10)E; (12)LR; (13)FR; (14)NB.

Rattoo:

(1)RP; (2)R; (3) 11000 feet; (4) 40 feet; (5)NEX; (6)NPB/R; (7)MSTM; (11)LR; (12)FR; (14B) nearby.

Roscommon:

Drift hill between two lakes. (5)EX.

The Augustinian abbey was situated on the site marked "Old Chapel" on the 1840 6″ O.S. map. It was situated on the north east edge of a former lake which occupied Ballypheasan townland and also a half mile south of Roscommon Castle, which is in Cloonbrackna townland. The castle was on the east edge of Loughaneane (present day football pitch) but land reclamation has reduced the water level so that the abbey which once stood on a site between two lakes does not show these features today. There is no river flowing into either of these lakes, nor river draining them, their existence was due to high water levels in the past.

Seir Kieran:

(1)RP; (2)L; (3) 450 feet; (4) 10 feet; (5)NE; (6)NPB/R; overlooking the floor plain. Topography of surrounding countryside rolling. (11)DS; (12) extensive earthworks. Evidence of early Celtic site. A 3–ring fort shown on 1840 O.S. map has been removed c.1968 by the Land Commission..

Saul:

(1)RP; (3) 390 feet; (7)D; (12)LR. On top of the greywacke is 10″ of boulder clay..

St. Wolstan's Celbridge:

(1)RP; (2)R; (3) 90 feet; (4) 40 feet; (5)EX; (7)MR; (11)DS; (12)LR; (14)NB.

Trim:

(1)RP; (2)L; (3) 20 feet; (4) 50 feet; (5)EX; (6)NPB/R; (7)MR; (12)FR; (14)NB.

Tristernagh:
> Lough Iron – shrunk – land reclamation scheme post 1930.
> Present day entrance via Ballynacarrigy. (5)EX. A landscape of
> red bog; (8)IB.

Tuam:
> (1)RP; (3) 3000 feet; abbey on top of ridge site marked by a gap
> in a street where there is frontage for three houses.

Abbeydorney:
> (1)RP; (2) south of the abbey is a small and sluggish stream,
> further north this stream becomes the Brick River, a tributary of
> the R. Feale. (8)IB; (11) low gravel ridge which juts out into
> black bog. (12)CR; local limestone and square blocks of red
> sandstone which appear on the exterior face of the west gable
> church 81 x 24 x 229 high; (14)B.

Abbeyknockmoy:
> (1)RP; (2)R; (3) 150 feet; (4) 15 feet; (5)EX; (6)PB/R; (7)MS;
> (9)RS; (11)DS thin veneer of glacial drift on limestone; (12)CR;
> (12)LR; (14) turbary one quarter of mile from abbey.

Abbeylara:
> (1)RP; (2)R; (3) 100 feet; (4) 3 feet; (5)EX; (6)NPB/R; (7)MS;
> (11)DS; (12)LR; (12)CR; (14)NB.

Abbeyleix:
> (1)RP; (2)R; (3) 75 feet; (4) 30 feet; (5)NEX; (6)NPB/R; (7)MR;
> (11)DS; (12)NER; (14)NB.

Abbeymahon Maure de fonte vive – but no evidence of spring today.
> (1)RP; (2)R; (3) 88 feet from sea shore; (5) exposure of greenish
> grey shales west of abbey site, grey sandy slates east of abbey.
> (8)M; (12)FR; (13) spot height 16 feet; (14)NB.

Abbeyshrule:
> (1)RP; (2)R; (3) 100 feet; (4) 40 feet; (5)EX; (7)MR; (11)DS;
> (12)LR; (14)NB.

Abbeystrowry:
> (1)RP; (2)R; (5)EX; (7)M; (8)M; (12)FR.

Abington:
> (1)RP; (2)R; (3) 264 feet; (4) 20 feet ; (5)EX; (7)MS; (12)LR
> limestone sandstone. There is a building in a graveyard two
> parts of which may be the south range of the former abbey;
> (14)NB.

Assaroe:

    (1)RP; (2)R; (3) 30 feet; (4) 15 feet; (5)EX; (6)PB/R; (7)MSTM; (11)DS; (12)LR; (12)FR; (14)NB.

Baltinglass:

    (1)RP; (2)L; (3) 264 feet; (4) 30 feet; (5)EX; (6)NPB/R; (7)MR; (10)E; (11)DS; (12)FR; (14)NB. The abbey was situated on a slight mound in the flood plain, sufficiently elevated to escape floods of 1904, and 1964. Regarding this site there are two possible theories: (1) There was a bend in the river but the monks diverted the stream unto its present course and thenceforth into the mill or (2) the river bifurcated to form an island on this island was the abbey. Evidence from higher water levels and rising water level as experience in 1904 and 1964, enabled the river to regain its old channel, thereby causing the abbey, present day rectory and some houses to be marooned. Rushes grow along this marshy bed to the east and west of the abbey. The rising ground to the east is called Sruthan. This site is at the junction of Leinster granite and limestone gravel although this is not exposed.

Bective:

    (1)RP; (2)L; (3) 300 feet; (4) 50 feet; (5)EX; (6)PB/R; (7)MR; (10)E; (11)DS; (12) R. Boyne sufficiently incised to expose the bed rock sandstone with thirty feet of morainic debris as overburden. (12)LR; (12)Considerable Remains; (fortified abbey); (14)NB.

Boyle:

    (1)RP; (2)L; (3) 88 feet; (4) 40 feet; (5)EX; (7)MR; (10)E; (11)DS; (12)CR; (14)NB.

Cashel:

    (1)RP; (2)R; (3) 300 feet; (4) 3 feet; (5)EX; (6)NPB/R; (7)MS; (10)NR; (11)DS; (12)LR; (12)CR; (14)NB; Flat ground at the foot of the rock promontory of Cashel, the stream floods, and there is marshy ground on either bank for about fifty yards.

Comber:

    (1)R; (3) 660 feet; (4) 20 feet; (5)NEX; (6)NPB/R; (7)MR; (8)D. The abbey is situated on a much dissected gravel terrace. Water was easy to obtain on account of the gravels. The solid rock is greywacke. To the south west is boulder clay. (134)NHE = 34' many drumlins over 509.

Corcumroe:

    (1)NRP; (5)EX; (8)M; (10)E; (11)DS; (12)LR; (12)CR; (13)NHE;

(14)NB. Abbey is less than one mile from the sea at Beala-clugga, and is not visible from the sea. Much of the land in the vicinity is Karst. Source for water is a well. No possibility of having a mill at the site. Priests' Valley contained some medium quality land.

Dunbrody:

(1)RP; (2)L; (3) 528 feet; (4) 15 feet; (5)NEX; (6)NPB/R; (7)NR; (10)E; (11)DS; (11)TD; over slate (12)LR; (14)NB.

Fermoy: (1)

(1)RP; (2)R; (3) 50 feet; (4) 40 feet; (6)NPB/R; (7)MR; (11)DS; (12)FR; (14)NB.

Graiguenamanagh:

(1)RP; (2)R; (3) 50 feet; (4) 40 feet; (5)EX; (6)PB/R; (7)MSTM; (10)E; (11)DS; (12)CR; There is a visible outcrop of schist in the Duiske Valley 220 yards from the abbey near the Fair Green. The abbey is at the foot of a steep glen where the R. Duiske flows into the R. Barrow.

Grey Abbey:

(1)NRP; (2) nearest river 1 mile south; (8)D; The Abbey is situated on thin boulder clay over greywacke (mainly grits and slates). There would be no chance of obtaining water through the boulder clay. Building stone is new red sandstone from ¾ mile distant. Water from Strangford Lough would be contaminated and saline.

Holy Cross:

(1)RP; (2)R; (3) 10 feet; (4) 60 feet; (5)EX; (6)PB/R; (7)MR; (10)E; (11)DS on river terrace; (12)CR; (14)NB.

Inch Abbey:

(1)RP; situated on the S.E. slope of a gentle drumlin, above a thin strip of river alluvium; (8)M; (10)E; (11)LR; (12)CR; (13)NHE; (14)NB.

Inishlounaght:

(1)RP; (2)L; (4) 40 feet; (5)EX; (6)PB/R; (7)MSTM; (12)NER; (14)NB.

A valley site with variation. The R. Suir is flowing from west to east and makes a pronounced bend at the Abbey turn, there is a lateral moranine (280') on the left bank of the Suir. A stream drained from Marfield Lake to the Suir, the Cistercians diverted this by making a new canal to drive their mill. The abbey was sited on the lower slope at a distance of 80' from the river. Solid rock is exposed to the north of the abbey.

Jerpoint:

(1)RP; (2)R; (3) 30 feet; (4) 9 feet; (5)NEX; (8)M; (10)E; (11)DS; The rock is thin limestone gravel over coarse sandstone of the Old Sandstone Age. (9)BS; (11)DS; The site is odd, being perched abover the river, which may be due to the Benedictine forerunner..

Kilbeggan:

(1)RP; (2)RB; (3) 50 feet; (5)NE; (6)NP/B; (7)M; (12)NER; (14)NB.

Macosquin:

(1)RP; (2)R; In Macosquin townland there is a strip of glacial sand and gravel; but Macosquin Abbey was sited to the west of the gravel belt on boulder clay/basalt. The boulder clay is ten feet deep. The river is not navigable; there are many basaltic rock barriers in the river bed..

Mellifont:

(1)RP; (2)L; (3) 30 feet; (4) 20 feet; (5)EX; (6)NPB/R; (7)MSTM; (10)E; (11)DS; (12)LR; (12)IM; (14)NB.

Middleton:

(1)RP; (2)L; (5)EX; (6)NPB/R; (7)M; (12)FR; (14)NB.

Monastereven:

(1)RP; (2)L; (3) 50 feet; (4) 40 feet; (5)NE; (6)NPB/R; (7)M; (12)FR; only one window of the north side of the cloister remains, this appears to have been built with carboniferous limestone. This is the flood plain of the R. Barrow. Fields on the left bank have damp pastures, water meadows. Three fields (360 yds. in width) of water meadows land along river side used for hay crop in summer only one crop is obtained. Bedded limestone overlain by limestone gravels and tills; mostly tills near the surface.

Monasternenagh:

(1)RP; (2)L; (3) 50 feet; (4) 30 feet; (5)EX; (6)PB/R; (7)MSTM; (10)E; (11)DS; (12)LR; (14)NB. Solid rock outcrops on site. This site is on a peneplain of limestone and slopes from NE to SW.

Newry:

(1)RP; (2)L; (3) 528 feet; (5)EX; (7)MR; (12)NER; (14)NB.

Tintern:

(1)RP; (2)L; (3) 120 feet; (4) 15 feet; (5)EX; (6)NPB/R; (7)MR; (12)CR; (14)NB.

Tracton:

(1)RP side valley of a mill stream fed from spring; (3) 176 feet; 1760 feet from sea; (5)EX; (6)NPB/R; (7)MS; (12)FR; (14)NB.

APPENDIX B

Geology of Sites

Abbey	Rock Type	Map Reference
Abbeymahon	greenish grey slates and grey sandy slates	Cork 136/2
Abbeystrowry	grits and slates	Cork 141/4
Ballinskelligs	red slaty grits	Kerry 97
Church Is. (Inchmacnerin)	red grits and conglomerates	
Dunbrody	thick drift over shale	Wexford 44/2
Ferns	slates volcanic ash	Wexford 15/2
Inistioge	slates sandstones grits	Kilkenny 32/2
Kells (Meath)	purple slates and grits	Meath 17/1
Louth Abbey	thick drift over grits and slates	Louth 11
Mellifont	blue grey flags and grits	Louth 23
Mothel	grits and slates	Waterford 3/7
Tintern	green grits slates	Wexford 45/3
Tracton	black slates near surface	Cork 99/3
Graiguenamanagh	schists	Kilkenny 29/2
Selskar	quartz	Wexford 37/4
Armagh	boulder clay over 10 feet thick on carboniferous limestone	Armagh 12
Bangor	boulder clay over greywacke grits and slates	Down 11
Clogher	drumlin slope boulder clay on carboniferous limestone	Tyrone 59
Clones	drumlin slope boulder clay on carboniferous limestone	Monaghan 12
Derry	boulder clay ten feet thick on Dalradian schists	Derry 20
Downpatrick (St. John's)	boulder clay over greygrits and slates	Down 31/38

106

Downpatrick (St. Thomas')	boulder clay over grey-wacke grits and slates	Down 30/37
Grey Abbey	boulder clay over grey-wacke grits and slates	Down
Inch	boulder clay over grey-wacke grits and slates	Down 30/31/37/38
Lorrha	boulder clay/gravel deposit	Tipperary 4
Macosquin	boulder clay ten feet thick on basalt	Derry 7/11
Movilla	boulder clay over grey-wacke grits and slates	Down 6
Saul	boulder clay over grey-wacke grits and slates	Down 31/38
Abbeyshrule	carboniferous limestone near the surface	Longford 23/4
Aghmacart	do.	Laois 34/2
Assaroe	do.	Donegal 107
Aughris	do.	Sligo 12/2
Ballysadare	do.	Sligo 20
Bridgetown	do.	Cork 34/2
Cahir	do.	Tipperary 75/4
Canon Is.	do.	Clare 60
Celbridge	do.	Kildare 11
Clare	do.	Clare 42/1
Cong	do.	Mayo 90/4
Corcomroe	do.	Clare 3/4
Devenish	do.	Fermanagh 22
Errew	do.	Mayo 38/4
Fertagh	do.	Kilkenny 8
Gill (Cork)	do.	Cork 74/3
Hare Is.	Carboniferous limestone near the surface	Longford 26
Holy Cross	do.	Tipperary 47/1
Hore	do.	Tipperary 83/1
Inishlounaght	do.	Tipperary 61
Innisfallen	do.	Kerry 66
Kells (Kilkenny)	do.	Kilkenny 27/2

Kilcooly	do.	Tipperary 43/3
Killeigh	do.	Galway 122/128
Knockmoy	do.	Kings 25
Lisgoole	do.	Fermanagh 27
Mayo	do.	Mayo 110
Middleton	do.	Cork 76/2/4
Navan	do.	Meath 25/3
Abbeyderg	thin drift carboniferous limestone near the surface	Longford 19/2
Aughrim	do.	Galway 87/2
Bective	do.	Meath 31/3
Clonfert	bog, drift not thick over carboniferous limestone	Galway 101/3
Killaha	thin drift carboniferous limestone near the surface	Kerry 47/3
Killeigh	do.	Offaly 25/3
Roscommon	do.	Roscommon 39/4
Seirkieran	do.	Offaly 39/1
Tristernagh	do.	Westmeath 11/1
Tuam	do.	Galway 29/4
Abbeydorney	fairly thick drift over carboniferous shales and sandstones	Kerry 21/2
Abbeyderg	thick drift over carboniferous limestone	Longford 9/2
Abbeygormacan	do.	Galway 107/1
Ballyboggan	do.	Meath 46/47
Ballymore	do.	Longford 10
Clonmacnoise	do.	Kings 56
Duleek	do.	Meath 27/3
Durrow	do.	Offaly 9/3
Kilbeggan	do.	Westmeath 38/1
Kilkenny	do.	Kilkenny 19/2
Kilmore	do.	Roscommon 12/18
Millingar	do.	Westmeath 19/3
Rathkeale	do.	Limerick 19/4
Rattoo	do.	Kerry 9

Abbeylara	blue grey flaggy carboniferous limestone	Longford 11/3
Abington	dark blue carboniferous limestone near the surface	Limerick 14/2
Ballybeg	pale grey limestone	Cork 17/3
Ballintober	black carboniferous limestone and shale.	Mayo 89/4
Inchcleraun	dark grey limestone with bands of chert	Longford 21
Inchmore	black cherty limestone	
Kilsħanny	drift thickness not known over grey flags	Clare 15/2
Monasternenagh	blue grey carboniferous limestone drift not thick	Limerick 31/4
Mohill	black flags carboniferous limestone	Leitrim32/4
Newtown Trim	black carboniferous limestone and shale	Meath 36/2
Saints Island L. Ree	dark grey thinly beeded crystalline limestone	Longford 26
Trim	black carboniferous limestone and shale	Meath36/2
Abbeyleix	very thick limestone gravel	Laois 23/4
Annaghdown	drift thickness not known over carboniferous limestone	Galway 56/69
Athassel	thin layer of alluvium over carboniferous limestone	Tipperary 68/1
Baltinglass	limestone gravel/schists/granite	Wicklow 26/27
Boyle	alluvium on carboniferous sandstone	Roscommon 6/3
Comber	dissected gravel terrace	Down 10
Corbally	limestone gravel over yellow sandstone	Tipperary 12
Dungiven	alluvium on carboniferous sandstone	Derry 24, 25, 31

Fermoy	river alluvium not thick over slates of Old Red Sandstone	Cork 35/2
Gallen	very thick limestone gravel	Offaly 14/4
Glendalough	drift	Wicklow 23
Great Connell	very thick limestone gravel	Kildare 23/4
Inchmore	drift thickness not known over carboniferous limestone	Longford 6
Jerpoint	thin limestone gravel over coarse Old Red Sandstone	Kilkenny 28/3
Kells	river terrace over basalt	Antrim 38/44
Monaincha	very thick limestone gravel	Tipperary 12/17
Monasterevan	drift thickness not known over carboniferous limestone	Kildare 26/27
Muckamore	gravel and sand moraine	Antrim 50
Naas	very thick limestone gravel	Kildare 23/4

APPENDIX C

1197   King Concobhar died in Boyle Abbey

1231   Dubhchabhlaigh daughter of Conchobhar MacDiarmada died.

1237   Gilla na nech o mannachain died

1244   Donnchadh interred in Boyle

1245   Conchobhar Ruad died

1253   Siulletan wife of Milidh MacGordelbh died

1264   Aenghus O'Clumhain bishop of Achonry died

1296   Gilla Isa Mac an Liathanaigh interred in Boyle

1297   Conchobhar interred in Boyle (King of Moylurg)

1313   Tadhg interred

1331   Maelrunaid MacDiarmada King of Magh Lurg died

1336   Tomaltach MacDiarmada King of Magh Lurg died

1343   Derbhail daughter of Aedh O'Domhnaill died

1307   Fachra O'Floinn interred

1343   Maelrunaidh Mor interred

1406   Tadhg MacDonnchaidh died

1407   Cathal O'Conchobar died in Boyle

1546   Ferghal son of Aedh interred in Boyle Abbey

1560   Maelrunaidh the Great interred

1582   Crimthann died in Boyle Abbey

1589   Conchobhar og died and was interred

Source: Annals of Loch Ce.

Boyle abbey had a hospital, these people died in Boyle Abbey presumably in the hospital. They may have given donations of land in recognition of this privilege.

COMMUNITY TRANSFERS

NAME	RANK	COUNTY	DATE FOUNDED osa	CONGREGATION
Armagh	Ab	Armagh	-1134 c.1140	Arrouaise
Ballysadare[1]	Ab	Sligo	-1166	AR
Bangor	Ab	Down	+ 1124, 1137 c.1140	AR
Clogher	Ab	Tyrone	+ 1140	AR
Clonard*	Ab	Meath	1146	AR
Clones	Ab	Monaghan	+ 1140	AR
Clonfert	Ab	Galway	+ 1140	AR
Clonmacnoise	Ab	Offaly	+ 1140	AR
Corbally	PR	Tipperary	c.1485	V. Monaincha
Derry	Ab	Derry	c.1233	
Devenish*	PR	Fermanagh	+ 1134 + 1440	AR*
Dublin Christ Ch.	CdPR	Dublin	c.1163	AR
St. Mary's Duleek	PR/Ab	Meath	+ 1140/c.1290	AR
Dungiven	PR	Derry	1140	A (?)
Elphin	PR	Roscommon	+ 1140	A (?)
Gallen	PR	Offaly	1140-8	A (?)
St. Kevin's Glendalough	Ab	Wicklow	+ 1163	A (?)
Hare Is.[2]	PR	Westmeath	+ 1140	
Inchcleraun	PR	Longford	+ 1140	A (?)
Inchmore*	PR	Longford	-1170	A*
Innisfallen	PR	Kerry	1197	
Killeigh*	PR	Offaly	+ 1144	A*
Lisgoole	Ab	Fermanagh	1140-8	A (?)
Louth[3]	CdPR	Louth	1140-8	A (?)
Lorrha	PR	Tipperary	1140	
Mayo	Ab	Mayo	c.1370	
Mohill*	PR	Leitrim	1216	*
Molana	PR	Waterford	1140	V. Corbally
Monaincha	PR	Tipperary	1140	
Mothel	PR	Waterford	+ 1140	A
Movilla[4]	Ab	Down	+ 1135 + 1140	A
Navan[5]	Ab	Meath	1170	A
Rattoo	Ab	Kerry	-1207	A
Roscommon	PR	Roscommon	1140	A
St. Michael Ballinskelligs	PR	Kerry	c.1210	A
Saints Is. L. Derg*	PR	Donegal	+ 1140	A*
Seirkieran	PR	Offaly	-1170	
Trim	Ab	Meath	+ 1140 -1186	A

TABLE 1

NOTES TO TABLE – COMMUNITY TRANSFERS

1. *Ballysadare*:

Early monastery founded by St. Feichin of Fore (d.665 or 668: Aa) Malefinnian coarb of Feichin (Ballysadare) and bp of Tuath—Luighne (Leyny, u Achonry) d.993. AU. An crenagh d.1158: AFM a coarb of Feichin and abbot of the monastery of the Canons of Es adara d.1230. AU. The Augustinian abbey of St. Mary and (St. Feichin) was built a short distance from the Church of the earlier monastery. No contemporary evidence has been found for the date of its foundation, which suggests that it was before the Anglo-Norman invasion, the titles erenagh and coarb continuing to be used.

Gwynne & Hadcock *Medieval Religious Houses* (1970), p. 160

2. *Hare Island*:

"The early monastery continued into the twelfth century and it may have become Augustinian some time after 1140. According to A716, the Dillons built a monastery here; perhaps a rebuilding of the early monastery some time after 1185. The main community was probably transferred from Hare Is. to the more convenient site on Saints Is., Co. Longford, when the large Augustinian priory of All Saints was founded by the Dillons before 1259."

Gwynn & Hadcock *Medieval Religious Houses* (1970), pp. 177–178

3. *Louth*:

"Augustinian rule was adopted at Louth probably when St. Malachy was legate 1140-8."

Gwynne & Hadcock *Medieval Religious Houses* (1970), pp. 185–186

4. *Movilla*:

"As at Bangor St. Malachy may have begun to introduce a form of the Augustinian rule at Movilla after 1135 and the Arrouasian observance after 1140."

Gwynn & Hadcock *Medieval Religious Houses* (1970), p.188

5. *Navan*:

"The Augustinian abbey of St. Mary may have taken the place of an earlier monastery q.v. Christian, ab. of Navan witnessed a charter of 1174–84; IEL 240. From this it can be presumed that the abbey was established before the Anglo-Norman invasion. John de Courcy confirmed the Ch. of St. Mary, Navan, to the regular canons serving God there 14 April, 5 (r.35) Henry II, i.e. 1189. Ware says that the abbey was either founded or restored by Jocelin Nangle (de Angulo) towards the end of the twelfth century."

Gwynn & Hadcock *Medieval Religious Houses* (1970), p. 189.

*Those marked thus * the Arrouasian Rule was
introduced from another abbey, and not by St. Malachy*

Devenish:
(Culdees in the
community)

"Ware says that a monastery was founded on this
island in 1130, but he was uncertain if this was a res-
toration of the early monastery or a new foundation.
The sixth century monastery of St. Molaise had Culdees, probably from the tenth century, and there can
be little doubt that the monastery founded in 1130 is
St. Mary's priory, which became a house of Augustinian canons. St. Mary's was probably colonized from
the abbey of SS Peter and Paul, Armagh, and it was
built a short distance away from the monastery of the
Culdees. It may have been hoped that these would
join the new priory, but though a few of the Culdees
became Augustinian they never came over in a body
so the two establishments continued side by side until
the suppression."

Gwynn & Hadcock *Medieval Religious Houses* (1970), p. 169.

Inchmore:
(late
foundation)

"The Augustinian rule, presumably of Arrouaise was
introduced and the early monastery became the priory of St. Mary, dependent on Louth." (for guidance)

Gwynn & Hadcock *Medieval Religious Houses* (1970), p. 179.

Killeigh:
(secular coarb
and late
foundation)

"Augustinian rule with the observances of Arrouaise
may have been adopted before St. Malachy's death
in 1148, or after the coarb's death in 1163, though
secular coarbs may have continued here as at several
other places. The early abbey became a priory, dependent on Durrow." (for guidance)

Gwynn & Hadcock *Medieval Religious Houses* (1970), pp. 182–83.

Mohill:
(late
foundation)

"Augustinian rule was introduced, possibly not until
after 1216 as the priory of St. Mary, Mohill is later
recorded to have been a dependency of Abbeyderg."
(for guidance)

Gwynn & Hadcock *Medieval Religious Houses* (1970), p. 187.

**Saints Is in
L. Derg:**
(secular coarb)

"Fd by St. Patrick or by St. Dabeoc, t. St. Patrick;
Another Patrick was Abbot in 850: Ware. W.H.
Grattan-Flood, in C.KE XII. 580, considers that St.
Patrick was founder and that St. Dabeoc presided
over the retreat 'St. Patricks' Pugatory in the sixth

century; he goes on to say that the monastery became a priory, dependent on abbey of SS Peter and Paul, Armagh for Augustinian canons in 1130 or 1134 Cilleni of L. Derg a. 722; Termon Dabeoc was pillaged by Ruaidri Ua Canannain in 1070: AU Hereditary coarbs continued in a secular capacity; from before 1247 Termon Dabeoc is known as Termon Mac-Raith, members of the Magrath family being coarbs in the thirteenth to sixteenth centuries: cf. AU and A. Conn. As at Armagh, the process of introducing the Augustinian rule may have begun a few years after c.1132 with the observance of Arrouaise after 1140. The foundation of the priory as a dependency of Armagh was probably due to St. Malachy: Dunning 303 Loch Derg Priory is named as belonging to Armagh Abbey in 1245 ratified 1322."

Gwynn & Hadcock *Medieval Religious Houses* (1970), p. 193.

116

Augustinian Abbeys
Refounded on abandoned Celtic sites

Name	Rank	County	Date Founded osa	Congregation
Aghmacart	PR	Laois	1168 (?)	
*Aughris	PR	Sligo	−1172 (?)	
Aughrim	PR	Galway	−1170 (?)	
*Canon Is.	Ab	Clare	c.1180	
Clontuskert O	PR	Galway	+1140	A
Cloontuskert	PR	Roscommon	+1140	A
Cong	Ab	Mayo	1134 (?) +1140	A
*Drumlane	PR	Cavan	1143–8	A*
Errew Pr.(Cl?)	PR	Mayo	1413?	
Fertagh	PR	Kilkenny	1251	
Inchmore	PR	Westmeath	−1170 +1200?	
Inistioge	PR	Kilkenny	c.1206	
Kells	Ab	Antrim	+1140	(A?)
Killaha	PR	Kerry	c.1216	
Kilmacduagh	Ab	Galway	1225–50	
Kilmore	PR	Roscommon	1232	
Muckamore	PR	Antrim	−1183	V
Saints Is. L. Ree	PR	Longford	−1200	
Saul	Ab	Down	+1140	A

Table 2

Name	Rank	County	Date Founded OSA	Congregation
Abbeyderg	PR	Longford	–1216	
Abbeygormacan	Ab	Galway	–1170	
Annaghdown*	Ab	Galway	+1140	A
Athassel	PR	Tipperary	c.1200	
Ballintober	Ab	Mayo	1216	
Ballybeg	PR	Cork	1229–37	
Ballyboggan	PR	Meath	–1200	
Ballymore	PR	W. Meath	c.1250	
Bridgetown	PR	Cork	1206–16	
Caher	PR	Tipperary	1200–20	
Clare	Ab	Clare	–1189	
Cork	Ab	Cork	1136–7	
Down	PR	Wexford	1170	
Downpatrick St. John's	PR	Down	+1140	
Downpatrick St. Thomas	PR	Down	–1183	
Dublin All Saints	PR	Dublin	c.1166	
Dublin St. Thomas	PR/Ab	Dublin	1177/1192	
Durrow	PR	Offaly	+1144	A
Glendalough St. Saviours	Ab	Wicklow	+1163	A(?)
Ferns	Ab	Wexford	c.1160–2	A
Great Connell*	PR	Kildare	1202	
Holmpatrick	PR	Dublin	1220	
Inchmacnerin	PR	Roscommon	1140–70	A(?)
Kells	Ab	Meath	1140–1186	
Kells*	PR	Kilkenny	1193	
Kilkenny	PR	Kilkenny	c.1202–1211	
Kilshanny	Ab	Clare	c.1194	
Knock	Ab	Louth	–1148	
Leighlin	PR	Carlow	+1163 c.1392	A(?)
Mullingar	PR	W. Meath	c.1227	
Naas	PR	Kildare	–1200	
Newtown Trim	Cd PR	Meath	1202	
Rathkeale	PR	Limerick	c.1210	(A)
St. Cath. Dublin	PR	Dublin	1219	
St. Wolstan's Dublin	PR	Kildare	c.1205	
Tristernagh	PR	W. Meath	c.1200	
Tuam	PR	Balway	c.1140	
Waterford St. Catherine	PR	Waterford	–1207	
Wexford	PR	Wexford	c.1190 +1216?	(S)?

Table 3

COMMUNITY TRANSFERS – CISTERCIANS

ABBEY	COUNTY	FOUNDATION	COLONIZED FROM
Dublin	Dublin	1139	Savigny O.S.B.
Cashel	Tipperary	1272	Mellifont (O.S.B. annexed)
Holy Cross	Tipperary	(1169?) 1180	Monasternenagh (O.S.B.)
Monasterevan	Kildare	(1178?) 1189	Baltinglass (O.S.B.)
Newry	Down	(–1148) 1153	Mellifont (O.S.B.)
Corcumroe	Clare	(1175?) 1195	Inishlounaght
Jerpoint	Kilkenny	1166–70	O.S.B.?
Kilcooly	Tipperary	c.1182	O.S.B.?

TABLE 4

ABANDONED CELTIC SITES CHOSEN BY CISTERCIANS

ABBEY	COUNTY	FOUNDATION	COLONIZED FROM
Abbeydorney	Kerry	1154	Monasternenagh
Comber	Down	1200	Wales (Whitland)
Inch	Down	1180	(Erenagh) Civiness
Kilbeggan	Westmeath	1150	Mellifont
Macosquin	Derry	1218	Morimond in France

TABLE 5

CISTERCIAN NEW SITES

ABBEY	COUNTY	FOUNDATION	COLONIZED FROM
Abbeyknockmoy	Galway	1190	Boyle
Abbeylara	Longford	1214	Dublin
Abbeyleix	Leix	1184	Baltinglass
Abbeymahon	Cork	(1172–1278)	Baltinglass (fr. Aghaminister)
Abbeyshrule	Longford	1200	Mellifont
Abbeystrowry	Cork	1228	Abbeymahon
Abington	Limerick	1204–1205	at Arklow Furness/Savigny
Assaroe	Donegal	1178	Boyle
Baltinglass	Wicklow	1148	Mellifont
Bective	Meath	1147	Mellifont
Boyle	Roscommon	1148	Mellifont
Dunbrody	Wexford	1182	Dublin
Fermoy	Cork	1170	Inishlounaght
Graiguenamanagh	Kilkenny	1202–4 (1204–7)	Stanley, Lough Merans, Annamult
Grey Abbey	Down	1193	Holmcultram
Inishlounaght	Tipperary	1147–8 (1151)	Mellifont
Mellifont	Louth	1142	Clairvaux
Middleton	Cork	1179	?
		1180	Monasternenagh
Monasternenagh	Limerick	1148	Mellifont
Tintern	Wexford	1200	Tintern (Wales)
Tracton	Cork	1225	Whitland (Wales)

TABLE 6

THE CELTIC INFLUENCE: ALTITUDE OF SITES

	50'	100'	200'	300'	400'	500'

Celtic Community Transfers: Augustinian	Ballysadare
	Bangor
	Clonard
	Devenish
	Dublin
	Elphin
	Lisgoole
	Molana
	Monaincha
	Rattoo
	St. Michael –
	  Ballinskelligs
		Clonfert
		Dungiven
		Innisfallen
			Clones
			Derry
			Duleek
			Gallen
			Hare Is.
			Inchcleraun
			Lorrha
			Louth
			Mohill
			Movilla
			Navan
			Roscommon
			Trim
				Armagh
				Clonmacnoise
				Inchmore
				  (Longford)
				Kells (A)
				Mayo
				Mothel
				Seirkieran
					Corbally
					Glendalough
					Killeigh
					Sts. Is.
					  L. Derg	

Celtic Abandoned Sites: Augustinian	Canon Is. Clontuskert Inchmore Killaha Sts. Is. L. Ree	Cong Errew Inistioge Kilmacduagh	Aughris Cloontuskert Kilmore	Aughrim Drumlane Saul	Aghmacart Muckamore	Fertagh
Celtic Community Transfers: Cistercians	Dublin Newry	Corcomroe Jerpoint	Monasterevan	Holy Cross Hore	Kilcooley	
Celtic Abandoned Sites: Cistercians	Abbeydorney Comber Inch Kilbeggan	Macosquin				

TABLE 7

ABSTRACTS FROM O'LOCHLAINN'S MAP
"ROADWAYS IN ANCIENT IRELAND"

SLIGE	ITINERARY	ITINERARY AND SLIGE	PROBABLE ROADS	MONASTERIES	FORTS-ROYAL SEATS	FORDS	TOWNS AND VILLAGES
Waterford	Camus Comber Ballyshannon Ballysadare Granard Ballintober Navan Duleek Cong Lorrha Cork	Kells Clonmacnoise Aughrim Naas Baltinglass Abbeyleix		Moville Kilkenny Derry Monasternenagh Bangor Clogher Downpatrick Armagh Cashel Newry Mellifont Kells Clonard Roscommon Tuam Celbridge Dublin Durrow Roscrea	Baltinglass		

TABLE 8

THE PHYSICAL CLASSIFICATION OF SITES:
AUGUSTINIAN ABBEYS

MAJOR RIVER	MINOR/MAJOR	MINOR STREAM	DRUMLINS	ISLANDS IN BOG OR IN THE SEA OR IN LAKES	MISCELLANEOUS
Athassel	Abbeydown	Abbeyderg	Armagh	Annaghdown	Aughris
Clare	Bridgetown	Abbeygormacan	Clogher	Canon Is.	Ballysadare
Clonard	Caher	Aghmacart	Clones	Clonfert	Bangor
Clontuskert	Cong	Aughrim	Drumlane	Derry	Clonmacnoise
Cloontuskert	Ferns	Ballintober	Downpatrick	Devenish	Corbally
Cork	Inistioge	Ballybeg	(St. John's)	Errew	Holmpatrick
Dublin	Kells (A)	Ballyboggan	Downpatrick	Hare Is.	Kilmacduagh
Dublin	Kells (Meath)	Ballymore	(St. Thomas')	Incheleraun	Kilshanny
Dublin	Killeigh	Duleek	Mohill	Inchmacnerin	Knock
Dungiven	Rathkeale	Durrow	Movilla	Inchmore	Roscommon
Gallen	Rattoo	Elphin	Saul	Inchmore	Selskar
Glendalough		Fertagh		Innisfallen	St. Michael Ballinskelligs
Glendalough		Kilmore		Killagh	Waterford
Great Connell		Lorrha		Molana	
Kells		Louth		Monaincha	
Kilkenny		Mayo		Saints Is. L. Derg	
Leighlin		Mothel		Saints Is. L. Ree	
Lisgoole		Naas		Tristernagh	
Muckamore		Seirkieran			
Mullingar		Tuam			
Navan					
Newtown Trim					
St. Catherine's Dublin					
St. Wolstan's					
Trim					

TABLE 9

THE PHYSICAL CLASSIFICATION OF CISTERCIAN ABBEY SITES

MAJOR RIVER	MINOR/MAJOR	MINOR STREAM	DRUMLINS	ISLANDS IN BOG OR IN THE SEA OR IN LAKES	MISCELLANEOUS
Abbeyleix	Assaroe	Abbeyknockmoy	Grey Abbey	Abbeydorney	Abbeystrowry
Abbeyshrule	Graiguenamanagh	Abbeylara			Corcomroe
Baltinglass	Inishlounaght	Abington			Inch
Bective	Mellifont	Cashel			Jerpoint
Boyle	Monasternenagh	Macosquin			Kilcooley
Comber		Tracton			Maure
Dublin					Middleton
Dunbrody					
Fermoy					
Holy Cross					
Kilbeggan					
Monasterevan					
Newry					
Tintern					

TABLE 10

THE PHYSICAL CLASSIFICATION OF SITES: AUGUSTINIAN NEW SITES

RIVER	ISLANDS IN LAKE OR IN THE SEA OR BOG	DRUMLIN	MISCELLANEOUS
Abbeyderg	Annaghdown	Downpatrick	Holmpatrick
Abbeygormacan	Inchmacnerin	(St. Thomas')	Kilshanny
Athassel	Tristernagh	Downpatrick	Knock
Ballintober		(St. John's)	St. Catherine's
Ballybeg			Waterford
Ballyboggan			Wexford
Ballymore			
Bridgetown			
Caher			
Clare			
Cork			
Down			
Dublin (All Saints)			
Dublin St. Thomas'			
Durrow			
Ferns			
Glendalough (St. Saviours)			
Great Connell			
Kells (M)			
Kells (K)			
Kilkenny			
Leighlin			
Mullingar			
Naas			
Newtown Trim			
Rathkeale			
St. Catherine's Dublin			
St. Wolstan's			
Tuam			

TABLE 11

THE PHYSICAL CLASSIFICATION OF SITES
CELTIC COMMUNITY TRANSFERS: AUGUSTINIANS

RIVER	ISLANDS IN LAKE OR IN THE SEA OR BOG	DRUMLIN	MISCELLANEOUS
Clonard	Clonfert	Armagh	Ballinskelligs
Dublin Christ Church	Derry	Clogher	Ballysadare
Duleek	Devenish	Clones	Bangor
Dungiven	Hare Is.	Mohill	Clonmacnoise
Elphin	Inchcleraun	Movilla	Corbally
Gallen	Inchmore L. Gowna		Roscommon
Glendalough (St. Kevins)	Innisfallen		
Killeigh	Molana		
Lisgoole	Monaincha		
Louth	Saints Is. L. Derg		
Lorrha			
Mayo			
Mothel			
Navan			
Rattoo			
Seirkieran			
Trim			

TABLE 12

REFOUNDED ON ABANDONED CELTIC SITES
AUGUSTINIAN ABBEYS

RIVER VALLEY	ISLANDS IN LAKE OR IN THE SEA OR BOG	DRUMLINS	MISCELLANEOUS
Aghmacart	Inchmore L. Ree	Drumlane	Aughris
Aughrim	Killagha	Saul	Kilmacduagh
Clontuskert	Sts. Is. L. Ree		
Cloontuskert	Canon Is.		
Cong	Errew		
Fertagh			
Inistioge			
Kells (A)			
Kilmore			
Muckamore			

TABLE 13

The Physical Classification of Sites
Cistercians New Sites

River Valley	Islands in lake or in the sea or bog	Drumlins	Miscellaneous
Abberknockmoy		Grey Abbey	Abbeymahon
Abbeylara			Abbeystrowry
Abbeyleix			Middleton
Abbeyshrule			
Abington			
Assaroe			
Baltinglass			
Bective			
Boyle			
Dunbrody			
Fermoy			
Graiguenamanagh			
Inishlounaght			
Mellifont			
Monasternenagh			
Tintern			
Tracton			

Table 14

THE PHYSICAL CLASSIFICATION OF SITES
COMMUNITY TRANSFERS: CISTERCIANS

RIVER	ISLANDS IN LAKE OR IN THE SEA OR BOG	DRUMLINS	MISCELLANEOUS
Dublin Hore Holy-Cross Monasterevan Newry			Corcomroe Jerpoint Kilcooly

TABLE 15

THE PHYSICAL CLASSIFICATION OF SITES
ABANDONED CELTIC SITES

RIVER	ISLANDS IN LAKE OR IN THE SEA OR BOG	DRUMLINS	MISCELLANEOUS
Comber Kilbeggan Macosquin	Abbeydorney		Inch

TABLE 16

Note: Tables 17 – 20 appear in the text, pp. 30–33.
Tables 21 – appear on pages 33 and 34.
Table 23 appears on page 51.

NOTES AND REFERENCES

1. A. Gwynn and R.N.Hadcock; *Medieval Religious Houses, Ireland* (Longman, 1970) Sources for the tabulae.

2. *Ibid*, p 123–44.

3. In Cistercian houses the superior, an abbot, appointed a prior who was responsible for discipline amongst the monks and remained in office as long as required; he was in fact a claustral prior. In Augustinian houses, the superior was sometimes an abbot, and sometimes a prior. In a priory the prior (*praepositus*) was elected by the community and was a conventual prior. Some Augustinian houses had abbots—Bangor, Ballintober, Abbeygormacan, Clonard, Armagh—; others had a prior—Ballybeg, Ballybogan and Bridgetown. In some abbeys attached to cathedrals, the first superior was abbot and also bishop, and the man appointed to look after the monks was called a prior.

4. The Cistercians did not have cells. The Augustinian cells were governed by priors, who were appointed and not elected. The priors of some priories were major superiors and could sit in parliament, but the prior of a cell had very little importance. Those cells included in Gwynn and Hadcock, pp. 198–200, are not included in this study.

5. E.G.Bowen, *Seaways, and Settlements in the Celtic Lands*. (Cardiff: University of Wales Press, 1969) p 128.

6. MacCoy Hayes, *Ulster and Other Early Maps c. 1600* (Irish Manuscript Commission, 1964).

7. This view has been challenged recently. It is claimed that the Norse were more interested in trade.

8. For details see pp. 102–109.

9. Gwynn and Hadcock, p. 145.

10. Gwynn and Hadcock. These tables have been compiled from this source. Sometimes it is not certain whether there was a community transfer to that of the new Order of not, in which case an asterisk has been placed beside the name of the abbey on the list and a footnote relating to each asterisk is included.

11. For the Cistercians the same method has been followed.

12. The word 'community' rather than Order was used in the early Middle Ages; it was not until Stephen Harding promulgated his constitutions and received papal approval that the word 'Order' was used.

13. Gwynn and Hadcock, pp. 146–52.

14. *Ibid.*, p 208–9.

15. *Ibid.*, p 201–2.

16. *Ibid.*, p 146.

17. *Ibid.*, p 146.

18. *Ibid.*

19. *Ibid.*, p. 149.

20. J.T.Gilbert (ed.), *Chartularies of St Mary's Abbey Dublin*. Vol. 1(a) (London: Longmans, 1884), and J.T.Gilbert (ed.), *Chartularies of St Mary's Abbey Dublin with The Register of its House at Dunbrody and Annals of Ireland*, (Vol. 11(b) London: Longmans):

'MXCLII. Mellifons fundatur' (*Chartularies*, Vol. 1 p 279, No. 255A)

The annals of the same abbey bear a like testimony; 'MXCLII Fundatur Abbatia Mellifontis, Donato Rege Urgallie Terras et poessiones donante, Malachia episcopo procurante, ad quam regendam Bernardus, Abbas Clarevallis misit Conventum de illis quos malachias in Aaravalle ad addiscendum ordinem reliquerat et postea miserat dato eis in Patrem Fratre Christiano, aduirigens deo uis quante sufficerant ad numerum abbatie que concepit et herperit quinque filis' (p. 262).

21. Gwynn and Hadcock; pp. 20–46.

22. A rath is a Celtic homestead, a farm of about thirty acres. In stony areas they were stone-walled; in other areas mud-walled. See drawing, p. 19.

23. D.McCourt 'The Dynamic Quality of Irish rural settlement', in R.H.Buchanan, (ed), *Man and His Habitat* (London: Routledge Keegan and Paul, 1971) p 151.

24. *Ibid.*

25. O'Corrain, *Ireland before the Normans*, The Gill History of Ireland (Dublin: Gill and Macmillan, 1972) Vol. 2, p. 72.

26. *Ibid.*

27. *Ibid.*

28. *Ibid.*, p. 88.

29. Andrew's, 'A Geographer's View of Irish History' in T.W.Moody and F.X.Martin. (edd.), *The Course of Irish History* (Cork: Mercier Press, 1967) 19–20.

30. *Ibid.*, p. 21.

31. C.O'Lochlainn, *Feil-Sgribhinn Mhic Neill/Roadways in Ancient Ireland* (Dublin: Colm O'Lochlainn, 1940) This map is abridged from MacLoclainn's map, p. 465.

32. E.G.Bowen, *Saints, Seaways and Settlements*, p. 138.

33. See pages 48–53 of this study for drumlin sites for windmills.

34. *Journal Royal Society of Antiquaries Ireland* Vol. 4, 5th Series (1894) p. 302.

35. By courtesy of the Board of Works, National Monuments Division, Dublin.

36. L.de Paor, 'Excavations at Mellifont Abbey Co. Louth, *Proceedings of the Royal Irish Academy*, 68 (1969) 131.

37. *Chartae Privilegia et Immunitates 18 Henry II to 18 Richard II (1171–1395)* Dublin: Irish Record Commission (1829–30).

38. W.Dugdale, *Monasticon Anglicanum*, second edition (1673) p. 1025.

39. This map has been abridged from G.H.Orpen, *Ireland under the Normans* Vol. I–II (1911); Vol. III–IV (1920) Oxford: Clarendon Press.

40. J.T.Gilbert, *Chartularies of St. Mary's Abbey Dublin* Vol. II (b).

41. Lough Ree is approximately thirty-nine square miles in area.

42. J.Ware, *De Hibernia, et civitatibus ejus*, (ed. of 1654, p. 206) says that the prior and convent finally moved to Corbally close by; M.Archdall, *Monasticon Hibernicium* (1786) says that this was because the canons found the vapours from the marshes surrounding the island unhealthy; in spite of the traditional salubrity and supernatural power of the isle.

32. T.Colby, *Ordnance Survey of the County of Londonderry* (Dublin: Hodges and Smith, 1837) p. 22

44 . Gwynn and Hadcock, 178.

45. P.Power *Journal Royal Society of Antiquaries of Ireland*, Vol. 2, 7th Series (1932) p. 142.

46. MacCoy Hayes, *Ulster and other early maps C. 1600.*

47. E.R.Norman and J.K.S.St. Joseph, *The Early Development of Irish Civilization* (Cambridge: University Press, 1969) p. 108.

48. There was a community at Jerpoint already. If a celtic community could survive there presumably the Cistercians could too.

1–2. Photos show Clonmacnoise (bottom) and the esker (top) that runs from it towards Dublin. (*Photographs: Cambridge University Collection. Copyright Reserved*)

134

3. Ballyboggan Abbey: A valley bottom site on the banks of the
   Boyne. Notice the esker and the road skirting the front of it. Similarly at Great Connell, Co. Kildare, at Cahir, Co. Tipperary, the road
   follows the tower limb of the esker. (*Cambridge University Collec-*
   tion: Copyright Reserved)

4. Athassel Abbey, Co. Tipperary: within a meander loop of one mile amplitude on the R. Suir. Notice the abandoned bridge over the millstream. The abbey domestic water supply was from the river, hence its nearness to the river bank. (*Cambridge University Collection: Copyright Reserved*)

5. Athassel Abbey: Five acres of monastic ruins, in the foreground the millstream. In 1280 the Prior was fined "for muddying the waters of the Suir" 10 marks. Perhaps this was the excavation that was in progress C.OD.1 No. 1740 1280.(*Photograph Courtesy of Commissioners of Public Works in Ireland*)

6. Cross section of one of the principal stone lined underground passages at Holy Cross Abbey. (*Photograph Courtesy of Commissioners of Public Works in Ireland*)

7. This part of the passage was especially opened for photography. A few feet inside the opening there had been a fall of masonry which almost completely blocked the passage. The water was at the same level as the nearby river which was then in flood, 4th March 1974. (*Courtesy of Commissioners of Public Works in Ireland*)

8. Stone vaulted conduit Ballintober. (*Courtesy of Commissioners of Public Works in Ireland*)

9. Kells Abbey, Co. Kilkenny: the surrounding land rising to two hundred feet forming an amphitheatre-like hollow on the banks of the King's River. (*Courtesy of Cambridge University Collection: Copyright Reserved*)

10. Kells was a fortified Abbey. Notice the curtain walls and the Seven
Turrets. The river has point bars and riffles. The mill was on the
right middle distance of the castellated or turret enclosure.
(*Courtesy of Commissioners of Public Works in Ireland*)

140

11. Inistioge, Co. Kilkenny. (*Courtesy of Commissioners of Public Works in Ireland*)

12. The Vale of Glendalough looking West. Valley site but elevated. Glendalough: the glen of the two lakes and incidentally the two monasteries St. Kevin's the Celtic site on the alluvial flat and St. Saviours on the eastern end of the valley on the lower lake, a new site. (*Cambridge University Collection: Copyright Reserved*)

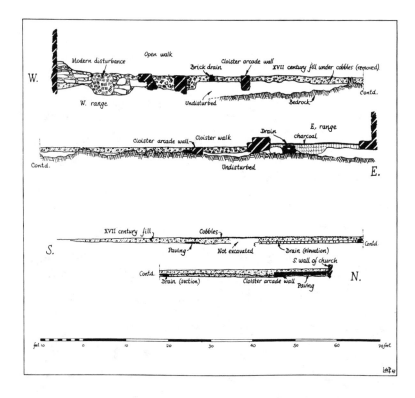

13. Mellifont Abbey, Co. Louth. Notice the drain revealed in the excavation. (*Courtesy of Commissioners of Public Works in Ireland*)

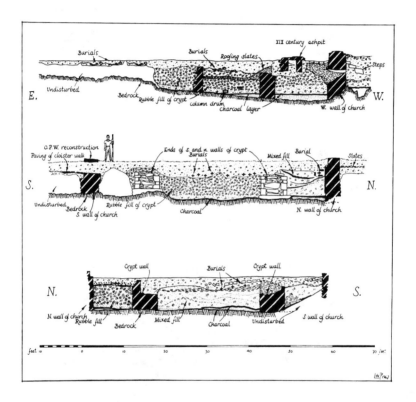

14. Mellifont Abbey, Co. Louth. (*Courtesy of Commissioners of Public Works in Ireland*)

144

15. Kells Abbey, Co. Kilkenny: Excavations 1972. The line of discoloration coincided with a layer of slates. A deed relating to the leasing of a slate quarry is recorded in the Calendar of Ormond Deeds 1348. (*Courtesy of Commissioners of Public Works in Ireland*)

16. Holy Cross Abbey: Excavations 1972 revealed the carboniferous limestone bed on which the abbey was raised. (*Courtesy of Commissioners of Public Works in Ireland*)

17. Boyle Abbey, Co. Roscommon. (*Cambridge University Collection: Copyright Reserved*)

18. Bective Abbey: Typical valley bottom site. (*Cambridge University Collection: Copyright Reserved*)

19. Inchcleraun: an island site, the mainland is visible. (*Courtesy of Commissioners of Public Works in Ireland*)

20. Inchcleraun from the air. The site is typical of an old Celtic site
(monastic) with an enclosing wall and a group of old churches inside it. Traces of the old dividing banks within the enclosure can be
seen. Changes in water level since the place was built possibly accounts for the three quarter circle of a wall backing onto the shore
rather than the usual complete enclosure. (*Cambridge University
Collection: Copyright Reserved*)

21. Monaincha, Co. Tipperary. (*Cambridge University Collection: Copyright Reserved*)

22. Errew Abbey, Co. Mayo: Notice (1) the extensive earthworks in the
foreground; (2) the ridge of cultivation; (3) the disturbed nature of
the buildings. (*Courtesy of Commissioners of Public Works in
Ireland*)

23. Errew Abbey, Co. Mayo: Viewed from the air. Notice the changed
shore line resulting from the National Drainage Scheme. (*Cambridge University Collection: Copyright Reserved*)

24. Movilla Abbey, Co. Down (Courtesy of the Ulster Museum).

25. Clogher Abbey, Co. Tyrone. (*Courtesy of The Northern Ireland Tourist Board*)

26. Corcomroe Abbey, Co. Clare: In the middle distance Priest's Valley. In the background the Burren. (*Courtesy of Commissioners of Public Works in Ireland*)

27. Inch Abbey, Co. Down: On the slope of a gentle drumlin. The land is sloping from the left of the picture to the right. The abbey overlooks the Quoile marshes. (*Courtesy of The Northern Ireland Tourist Board*)

154

28. Grey Abbey, Co. Down: On the slope of a gentle drumlin. An un-
Cistercian-like Abbey site, with no river near. (*Courtesy of The
Northern Ireland Tourist Board*)

29. Kilcooley Cistercian Abbey, Co. Tipperary, an unusual siting for a
Cistercian Abbey at four hundred feet and no river in its vicinity.
(*Cambridge University Collection: Copyright Reserved*)

30. Kilmacduagh Abbey, Co. Galway: Notice the limestone outcrops
in the fore-ground. In winter when the water table rises these limestone outcrops are covered with water. In summer when the water
table falls the lakes disappear, therefore for part of the year this site
may be marooned and may be described as an island surrounded by
turloughs. Nevertheless firm ground between the turloughs allows
approach to the east. (*Courtesy of Commissioners of Public Works
in Ireland*)

31. An aerial view of Kilmacduagh. Notice (1) on top left of photograph at "X" a remaining turlough, (2) cereal cultivation. (*Cambridge University Collection: Copyright Reserved*)

158

32. Jerpoint Abbey, Co. Kilkenny: an elevated site may be described as an abbey on a Fall line. This was a celtic site on the right bank of the Arrigle River and avoids the main river the Nore which with a low head at this point has a tendency to flood. Notice the re-entrant stream in the fore-ground. (*Cambridge University Collection: Copyright Reserved*)

CISTERCIAN PUBLICATIONS INC.

TITLES LISTING

THE CISTERCIAN FATHERS SERIES

THE WORKS OF BERNARD OF CLAIRVAUX

Treatises I: Apologia to Abbot William,
On Precept and Dispensation . . . . CF 1

On the Song of Songs I–IV . . CF 4, 7, 31, 40

The Life and Death of Saint Malachy
the Irishman . . . . CF 10

Treatises II: The Steps of Humility,
On Loving God . . . . CF 13

Magnificat: Homilies in Praise of the
Blessed Virgin Mary [with Amadeus
of Lausanne] . . . . CF 18

Treatises III: On Grace and Free Choice,
In Praise of the New Knighthood CF 19

Sermons on Conversion: A Sermon to
Clerics, Lenten Sermons on
Psalm 91 . . . . CF 25

Five Books on Consideration:
Advice to A Pope . . . . CF 37

THE WORKS OF WILLIAM OF SAINT THIERRY

On Contemplating God, Prayer,
and Meditations . . . . CF 3

Exposition on the Song of Songs . . . CF 6

The Enigma of Faith . . . . CF 9

The Golden Epistle . . . . CF 12

The Mirror of Faith . . . . CF 15

Exposition on the Epistle to the
Romans . . . . CF 27

The Nature and Dignity of Love . . CF 30

THE WORKS OF AELRED OF RIEVAULX

Treatises I: On Jesus at the Age of
Twelve, Rule for a Recluse,
The Pastoral Prayer . . . . CF 2

Spiritual Friendship . . . . CF 5

The Mirror of Charity . . . . CF 17†

Dialogue on the Soul . . . . CF 22

THE WORKS OF GILBERT OF HOYLAND

Sermons on the Song of Songs
I–III . . . . CF 14, 20, 26

Treatises, Sermons, and Epistles . . CF 34

OTHER EARLY CISTERCIAN WRITERS

The Letters of Adam of Perseigne, I . CF 21

Alan of Lille: The Art of Preaching . CF 23

John of Ford. Sermons on the Final
Verses of the Song of Songs,
I–IV . . . . CF 29, 39, 43, 44

Idung of Prüfening. Cistercians and
Cluniacs: The Case for Cîteaux . . CF 33

The Way of Love . . . . CF 16

Guerric of Igny. Liturgical Sermons
I–II . . . . CF 8, 32

Three Treatises on Man: A Cistercian
Anthropology . . . . CF 24

Isaac of Stella. Sermons on the
Christian Year, I . . . . CF 11

Stephen of Lexington. Letters from
Ireland . . . . CF 28

THE CISTERCIAN STUDIES SERIES

MONASTIC TEXTS

Evagrius Ponticus. Praktikos and
Chapters on Prayer . . . . CS 4

The Rule of the Master . . . . CS 6

The Lives of the Desert Fathers . . . CS 34

Dorotheos of Gaza. Discourses and
Sayings . . . . CS 33

Pachomian Koinona I–III:
The Lives . . . . CS 45
The Chronicles and Rules . . . . . CS 46
The Instructions, Letters and Other
Writings of St Pachomius and
His Disciples . . . . CS 47

* Temporarily out of print   † Forthcoming

Symeon the New Theologian. Theological and Practical Treatises and
Three Theological Discourses . . . cs 41

Guigo II the Carthusian. The Ladder
of Monks and Twelve Meditations . cs48

The Monastic Rule of
Iosif Volotsky . . . . cs 36

CHRISTIAN SPIRITUALITY

The Spirituality of Western
Christendom . . . . cs 30

Russian Mystics (Sergius Bolshakoff) cs 26

In Quest of the Absolute: The Life and
Works of Jules Monchanin
(J. G. Weber) . . . . cs 51

The Name of Jesus
(Irenée Hausherr) . . . . cs 44

Entirely for God: A Life of Cyprian
Tansi (Elizabeth Isichei) . . . . cs 43

Abba: Guides to Wholeness and
Holiness East and West . . . . cs 38

MONASTIC STUDIES

The Abbot in Monastic Tradition
(Pierre Salmon) . . . . cs 14

Why Monks? (François
Vandenbroucke) . . . . cs 17

Silence in the Rule of St Benedict
(Ambrose Wathen) . . . . cs 22

One Yet Two: Monastic Tradition
East and West . . . . cs 29

Community and Abbot in the Rule of St
Benedict I (Adalbert de Vogüé) . cs 5/1

Consider Your Call: A Theology of the
Monastic Life (Daniel Rees et al) . cs 20

Households of God (David Parry) . . cs 39

CISTERCIAN STUDIES

The Cistercian Spirit
(M. Basil Pennington, ed.) . . . . . . cs 3

The Eleventh-Century Background of
Cîteaux (Bede K. Lackner) . . . . . . cs 8

Contemplative Community . . . . cs 21

Cistercian Sign Language
(Robert Barakat) . . . . cs 11

The Cistercians in Denmark
(Brian P. McGuire) . . . . cs 35

Saint Bernard of Clairvaux: Essays
Commemorating the Eighth
Centenary of His Canonization . . cs 28

Bernard of Clairvaux: Studies Presented
to Dom Jean Leclercq . . . . cs 23

Bernard of Clairvaux and the Cistercian
Spirit (Jean Leclercq) . . . . cs 16

William of St Thierry: The Man and
His Work (J. M. Déchanet) . . . . cs 10

Aelred of Rievaulx: A Study
(Aelred Squire) . . . . cs 50

Christ the Way: The Christology of
Guerric of Igny (John Morson) . . cs 25

The Golden Chain: The Theological
Anthropology of Isaac of Stella
(Bernard McGinn) . . . . cs 15

Studies in Cistercian Art and Archi-
tecture, I (Meredith Lillich, ed) . . cs 66

*Studies in Medieval Cistercian
History sub-series*

Studies I . . . . cs 13

Studies II . . . . cs 24

Cistercian Ideals and Reality
(Studies III) . . . . . : . . . . cs 60

Simplicity and Ordinariness
(Studies IV) . . . . cs 61

The Chimera of His Age: Studies on
St Bernard (Studies V) . . . . cs 63

Cistercians in the Late Middle Ages
(Studies VI) . . . . cs 64

Noble Piety and Reformed Monasticism
(Studies VII) . . . . cs 65

Benedictus: Studies in Honor of St
Benedict of Nursia (Studies VIII) . cs 67

Heaven on Earth (Studies IX) . . . . cs 68†

THOMAS MERTON

The Climate of Monastic Prayer . . . . cs 1

Thomas Merton on St Bernard . . . . . cs 9

Thomas Merton's Shared Contemplation: A Protestant Perspective
(Daniel J. Adams) . . . . cs 62

Solitude in the Writings of Thomas Merton
(Richard Anthony Cashen) . . . . cs 40

The Message of Thomas Merton
(Brother Patrick Hart, ed.) . . . . . cs 42

FAIRACRES PRESS, OXFORD

The Wisdom of the Desert Fathers

The Letters of St Antony the Great

The Letters of Ammonas, Successor of
St Antony

A Study of Wisdom. Three Tracts by the
author of *The Cloud of Unknowing*

The Power of the Name. The Jesus
Prayer in Orthodox Spirituality
(Kallistos Ware)

Solitude and Communion

Contemporary Monasticism

A Pilgrim's Book of Prayers
(Gilbert Shaw)

Theology and Spirituality (Andrew Louth)

* *Temporarily out of print*   † *Forthcoming*